Selected Speeches
of
Barack Obama

Selected Speeches
of
Barack Obama

APPLEWOOD BOOKS
Carlisle, Massachusetts

© 2018 Applewood Books, Inc.

Thank you for purchasing an Applewood book.
Applewood reprints America's lively classics—books
from the past that are still of interest to modern readers.
For a free copy of our current catalog, please write to:
Applewood Books, P.O. Box 27, Carlisle, MA 01741.

ISBN 978-1-4290-9446-7

MANUFACTURED IN
THE UNITED STATES OF AMERICA

TABLE OF CONTENTS

Keynote Address at the Democratic National Convention 5
A More Perfect Union 13
Acceptance Speech at the Democratic National Convention 29
First Inaugural Address 45
A New Beginning 53
Acceptance of the Nobel Peace Prize 71
Tucson Memorial Speech 85
Economics Speech in Osawatomie 95
Remarks on the Sandy Hook Elementary Shootings 113
Second Inaugural Address 119
Remarks at the 50th Anniversary of the Selma Marches 127
Charleston Shooting Eulogy 139
Commencement Address at Rutgers University 143
Democratic National Convention Speech 159
Dedication of the National Museum of African American
      History and Culture 173
Farewell Address 183

Keynote Address

DEMOCRATIC NATIONAL CONVENTION
BOSTON, MASSACHUSETTS
TUESDAY, JULY 27, 2004

ON BEHALF OF the great state of Illinois, crossroads of a nation, land of Lincoln, let me express my deep gratitude for the privilege of addressing this convention. Tonight is a particular honor for me because, let's face it, my presence on this stage is pretty unlikely. My father was a foreign student, born and raised in a small village in Kenya. He grew up herding goats, went to school in a tin-roof shack. His father, my grandfather, was a cook, a domestic servant.

But my grandfather had larger dreams for his son. Through hard work and perseverance my father got a scholarship to study in a magical place: America, which stood as a beacon of freedom and opportunity to so many who had come before. While studying here, my father met my mother. She was born in a town on the other side of the world, in Kansas. Her father worked on oil rigs and farms through most of the Depression. The day after Pearl Harbor he signed up for duty, joined Patton's army and marched across Europe. Back home, my grandmother raised their baby and went to work on a bomber assembly line. After the war, they studied on the GI Bill, bought a house through FHA, and moved west in search of opportunity.

And they, too, had big dreams for their daughter, a common dream, born of two continents. My parents shared not only an improbable love; they shared an abiding faith in the possibilities of this nation. They would give me an African name, Barack, or "blessed," believing that in a tolerant America your name is no barrier to success. They imagined me going to the best schools in the land, even though they weren't rich, because in a generous America you don't have to be rich to achieve your potential. They are both passed away now. Yet, I know that, on this night, they look down on me with pride.

I stand here today, grateful for the diversity of my heritage, aware that my parents' dreams live on in my precious daughters. I stand here knowing that my story is part of the larger American story, that I owe a debt to all of those who came before me, and that, in no other country on earth, is my story even possible. Tonight, we gather to affirm the greatness of our nation, not because of the height of our skyscrapers, or the power of our military, or the size of our economy. Our pride is based on a very simple premise, summed up in a declaration made over two hundred years ago, "We hold these truths to be self-evident, that all men are created equal. That they are endowed by their Creator with certain inalienable rights. That among these are life, liberty and the pursuit of happiness."

That is the true genius of America, a faith in the simple dreams of its people, the insistence on small miracles. That we can tuck in our children at night and know they are fed and clothed and safe from harm. That we can say what we think, write what we think, without hearing a sudden knock on the door. That we can have an idea and start our own business without paying a bribe or hiring somebody's son. That we can participate in the political process without fear of retribution, and that our votes will be counted—or at least, most of the time.

This year, in this election, we are called to reaffirm our values and commitments, to hold them against a hard reality and see how we are measuring up, to the legacy of our forebearers, and the promise of future generations. And fellow Americans? Democrats, Republicans, Independents? I say to you tonight: we have more work to do. More to do for the workers I met in Galesburg, Illinois, who are losing their union jobs at the Maytag plant that's moving to Mexico, and now are having to compete with their own children for jobs that pay seven bucks an hour. More to do for the father I met who was losing his job and choking back tears, wondering how he would pay $4,500 a month for the drugs his son needs without the health benefits he counted on. More to do for the young woman in East St. Louis, and thousands more like her, who has the grades, has the drive, has the will, but doesn't have the money to go to college.

Don't get me wrong. The people I meet in small towns and big cities, in diners and office parks, they don't expect government to solve all their problems. They know they have to work hard to get ahead and they want to. Go into the collar counties around Chicago, and people will tell you they don't want their tax money wasted by a welfare agency or the Pentagon. Go into any inner city neighborhood, and folks will tell you that government alone can't teach kids to learn. They know that parents have to parent, that children can't achieve unless we raise their expectations and turn off the television sets and eradicate the slander that says a black youth with a book is acting white. No, people don't expect government to solve all their problems. But they sense, deep in their bones, that with just a change in priorities, we can make sure that every child in America has a decent shot at life, and that the doors of opportunity remain open to all. They know we can do better. And they want that choice.

In this election, we offer that choice. Our party has chosen a man to lead us who embodies the best this country has to offer. That man is John Kerry. John Kerry understands the ideals of community, faith, and sacrifice, because they've defined his life. From his heroic service in Vietnam to his years as prosecutor and lieutenant governor, through two decades in the United States Senate, he has devoted himself to this country. Again and again, we've seen him make tough choices when easier ones were available. His values and his record affirm what is best in us.

John Kerry believes in an America where hard work is rewarded. So instead of offering tax breaks to companies shipping jobs overseas, he'll offer them to companies creating jobs here at home. John Kerry believes in an America where all Americans can afford the same health coverage our politicians in Washington have for themselves. John Kerry believes in energy independence, so we aren't held hostage to the profits of oil companies or the sabotage of foreign oil fields. John Kerry believes in the constitutional freedoms that have made our country the envy of the world, and he will never sacrifice our basic liberties nor use faith as a wedge to divide us. And John Kerry believes that in a dangerous world, war must be an option, but it should never be the first option.

A while back, I met a young man named Shamus at the VFW Hall in East Moline, Illinois. He was a good-looking kid, six-two or six-three, clear-eyed, with an easy smile. He told me he'd joined the Marines and was heading to Iraq the following week. As I listened to him explain why he'd enlisted, his absolute faith in our country and its leaders, his devotion to duty and service, I thought this young man was all any of us might hope for in a child. But then I asked myself: Are we serving Shamus as well as he was serving us? I thought of more than 900 service men and women, sons and daughters, husbands and wives, friends and neighbors, who will not be returning to their hometowns. I thought of families I had met who were struggling to get by without a loved one's full income, or whose loved ones had returned with a limb missing or with nerves shattered, but who still lacked long-term health benefits because they were reservists. When we send our young men and women into harm's way, we have a solemn obligation not to fudge the numbers or shade the truth about why they're going, to care for their families while they're gone, to tend to the soldiers upon their return, and to never ever go to war without enough troops to win the war, secure the peace, and earn the respect of the world.

Now let me be clear. We have real enemies in the world. These enemies must be found. They must be pursued and they must be defeated. John Kerry knows this. And just as Lieutenant Kerry did not hesitate to risk his life to protect the men who served with him in Vietnam, President Kerry will not hesitate one moment to use our military might to keep America safe and secure. John Kerry believes in America. And he knows it's not enough for just some of us to prosper. For alongside our famous individualism, there's another ingredient in the American saga.

A belief that we are connected as one people. If there's a child on the south side of Chicago who can't read, that matters to me, even if it's not my child. If there's a senior citizen somewhere who can't pay for her prescription and has to choose between medicine and the rent, that makes my life poorer, even if it's not my grandmother. If there's an Arab American family being rounded up without benefit of an attorney or due process, that threatens my civil liberties. It's that fundamental belief—I am my brother's keeper, I am my sister's keeper—that makes this country work. It's what allows us to pursue our individual dreams, yet still come together as a single American family. "*E pluribus unum.*" Out of many, one.

Yet even as we speak, there are those who are preparing to divide us, the spin masters and negative ad peddlers who embrace the politics of anything goes. Well, I say to them tonight, there's not a liberal America and a conservative America; there's the United States of America. There's not a black America and white America and Latino America and Asian America; there's the United States of America. The pundits like to slice-and-dice our country into Red States and Blue States; Red States for Republicans, Blue States for Democrats. But I've got news for them, too. We worship an awesome God in the Blue States, and we don't like federal agents poking around our libraries in the Red States. We coach Little League in the Blue States and have gay friends in the Red States. There are patriots who opposed the war in Iraq and patriots who supported it. We are one people, all of us pledging allegiance to the stars and stripes, all of us defending the United States of America.

In the end, that's what this election is about. Do we participate in a politics of cynicism or a politics of hope? John Kerry calls on us to hope. John Edwards calls on us to hope. I'm not talking about blind optimism here, the almost willful ignorance that thinks unemployment will go away if we just don't talk about it, or the health care crisis will solve itself if we just ignore it. No, I'm talking about something more substantial. It's the hope of slaves sitting around a fire singing freedom songs; the hope of immigrants setting out for distant shores; the hope of a young naval lieutenant bravely patrolling the Mekong Delta; the hope of a millworker's son who dares to defy the odds; the hope of a skinny kid with a funny name who believes that America has a place for him, too. The audacity of hope!

In the end, that is God's greatest gift to us, the bedrock of this nation; the belief in things not seen; the belief that there are better days ahead. I believe we can give our middle class relief and provide working families with a road to opportunity. I believe we can provide jobs to the jobless, homes to the homeless, and reclaim young people in cities across America from violence and despair. I believe that as we stand on the crossroads of history, we can make the right choices, and meet the challenges that face us. America!

Tonight, if you feel the same energy I do, the same urgency I do, the same passion I do, the same hopefulness I do—if we do what we must do, then I have no doubt that all across the country, from Florida to Oregon, from Washington to Maine, the people will rise up in November, and John Kerry will be sworn in as president, and John Edwards will be sworn in as vice president, and this country will reclaim its promise, and out of this long political darkness a brighter day will come. Thank you and God bless you.

A More Perfect Union

"THE RACE SPEECH"
PHILADELPHIA, PENNSYLVANIA
TUESDAY, MARCH 18, 2008

"We the people, in order to form a more perfect union."

TWO HUNDRED AND TWENTY-ONE years ago, in a hall that still stands across the street, a group of men gathered and, with these simple words, launched America's improbable experiment in democracy. Farmers and scholars, statesmen and patriots who had traveled across an ocean to escape tyranny and persecution finally made real their declaration of independence at a Philadelphia convention that lasted through the spring of 1787.

The document they produced was eventually signed but ultimately unfinished. It was stained by this nation's original sin of slavery, a question that divided the colonies and brought the convention to a stalemate until the founders chose to allow the slave trade to continue for at least twenty more years, and to leave any final resolution to future generations.

Of course, the answer to the slavery question was already embedded within our Constitution—a Constitution that had at its very core the ideal of equal citizenship under the law; a Constitution that promised its people liberty, and justice, and a union that could be and should be perfected over time.

And yet words on a parchment would not be enough to deliver slaves from bondage, or provide men and women of every color and creed their full rights and obligations as citizens of the United States. What would be needed were

Americans in successive generations who were willing to do their part—through protests and struggle, on the streets and in the courts, through a civil war and civil disobedience and always at great risk—to narrow that gap between the promise of our ideals and the reality of their time.

This was one of the tasks we set forth at the beginning of this campaign—to continue the long march of those who came before us, a march for a more just, more equal, more free, more caring and more prosperous America. I chose to run for the presidency at this moment in history because I believe deeply that we cannot solve the challenges of our time unless we solve them together—unless we perfect our union by understanding that we may have different stories, but we hold common hopes; that we may not look the same and we may not have come from the same place, but we all want to move in the same direction—towards a better future for our children and our grandchildren.

This belief comes from my unyielding faith in the decency and generosity of the American people. But it also comes from my own American story.

I am the son of a black man from Kenya and a white woman from Kansas. I was raised with the help of a white grandfather who survived a Depression to serve in Patton's Army during World War II and a white grandmother who worked on a bomber assembly line at Fort Leavenworth while he was overseas. I've gone to some of the best schools in America and lived in one of the world's poorest nations. I am married to a black American who carries within her the blood of slaves and slave owners—an inheritance we pass on to our two precious daughters. I have brothers, sisters, nieces, nephews, uncles and cousins, of every race and every hue, scattered across three continents, and for as long as I live, I will never forget that in no other country on Earth is my story even possible.

It's a story that hasn't made me the most conventional candidate. But it is a story that has seared into my genetic makeup the idea that this nation is more than the sum of its parts—that out of many, we are truly one.

Throughout the first year of this campaign, against all predictions to the contrary, we saw how hungry the American people were for this message of unity. Despite the temptation to view my candidacy through a purely racial lens, we won commanding victories in states with some of the whitest populations in the country. In South Carolina, where the Confederate flag still flies, we built a powerful coalition of African Americans and white Americans.

This is not to say that race has not been an issue in the campaign. At various stages in the campaign, some commentators have deemed me either "too black" or "not black enough." We saw racial tensions bubble to the surface during the week before the South Carolina primary. The press has scoured every exit poll for the latest evidence of racial polarization, not just in terms of white and black, but black and brown as well.

And yet, it has only been in the last couple of weeks that the discussion of race in this campaign has taken a particularly divisive turn.

On one end of the spectrum, we've heard the implication that my candidacy is somehow an exercise in affirmative action; that it's based solely on the desire of wide-eyed liberals to purchase racial reconciliation on the cheap. On the other end, we've heard my former pastor, Reverend Jeremiah Wright, use incendiary language to express views that have the potential not only to widen the racial divide, but views that denigrate both the greatness and the goodness of our nation; that rightly offend white and black alike.

I have already condemned, in unequivocal terms, the statements of Reverend Wright that have caused such controversy. For some, nagging questions remain. Did I know him to be an occasionally fierce critic of American domestic and foreign policy? Of course. Did I ever hear him make remarks that could be considered controversial while I sat in church? Yes. Did I strongly disagree with many of his political views? Absolutely—just as I'm sure many of you have heard remarks from your pastors, priests, or rabbis with which you strongly disagreed.

But the remarks that have caused this recent firestorm weren't simply controversial. They weren't simply a religious leader's effort to speak out against perceived injustice. Instead, they expressed a profoundly distorted view of this country—a view that sees white racism as endemic, and that elevates what is wrong with America above all that we know is right with America; a view that sees the conflicts in the Middle East as rooted primarily in the actions of stalwart allies like Israel, instead of emanating from the perverse and hateful ideologies of radical Islam.

As such, Reverend Wright's comments were not only wrong but divisive, divisive at a time when we need unity; racially charged at a time when we need to come together to solve a set of monumental problems—two wars, a terrorist threat, a falling economy, a chronic health care crisis and potentially devastating climate change; problems that are neither black or white or Latino or Asian, but rather problems that confront us all.

Given my background, my politics, and my professed values and ideals, there will no doubt be those for whom my statements of condemnation are not enough. Why associate myself with Reverend Wright in the first place, they may ask? Why not join another church? And I confess that if all that I knew of Reverend Wright were the snippets of those sermons that have run in an endless loop on the television and

YouTube, or if Trinity United Church of Christ conformed to the caricatures being peddled by some commentators, there is no doubt that I would react in much the same way.

But the truth is, that isn't all that I know of the man. The man I met more than twenty years ago is a man who helped introduce me to my Christian faith, a man who spoke to me about our obligations to love one another; to care for the sick and lift up the poor. He is a man who served his country as a U.S. Marine; who has studied and lectured at some of the finest universities and seminaries in the country, and who for over thirty years led a church that serves the community by doing God's work here on Earth—by housing the homeless, ministering to the needy, providing day care services and scholarships and prison ministries, and reaching out to those suffering from HIV/AIDS.

In my first book, *Dreams from My Father*, I described the experience of my first service at Trinity:

"People began to shout, to rise from their seats and clap and cry out, a forceful wind carrying the reverend's voice up into the rafters....And in that single note—hope!—I heard something else; at the foot of that cross, inside the thousands of churches across the city, I imagined the stories of ordinary black people merging with the stories of David and Goliath, Moses and Pharaoh, the Christians in the lion's den, Ezekiel's field of dry bones. Those stories—of survival, and freedom, and hope—became our story, my story; the blood that had spilled was our blood, the tears our tears; until this black church, on this bright day, seemed once more a vessel carrying the story of a people into future generations and into a larger world. Our trials and triumphs became at once unique and universal, black and more than black; in chronicling our journey, the stories and songs gave us a means to reclaim memories that we didn't need to feel shame about...memories that all people might study and cherish—and with which we could start to rebuild."

That has been my experience at Trinity. Like other predominantly black churches across the country, Trinity embodies the black community in its entirety—the doctor and the welfare mom, the model student and the former gangbanger. Like other black churches, Trinity's services are full of raucous laughter and sometimes bawdy humor. They are full of dancing, clapping, screaming and shouting that may seem jarring to the untrained ear. The church contains in full the kindness and cruelty, the fierce intelligence and the shocking ignorance, the struggles and successes, the love and yes, the bitterness and bias that make up the black experience in America.

And this helps explain, perhaps, my relationship with Reverend Wright. As imperfect as he may be, he has been like family to me. He strengthened my faith, officiated my wedding, and baptized my children. Not once in my conversations with him have I heard him talk about any ethnic group in derogatory terms, or treat whites with whom he interacted with anything but courtesy and respect. He contains within him the contradictions—the good and the bad—of the community that he has served diligently for so many years.

I can no more disown him than I can disown the black community. I can no more disown him than I can my white grandmother—a woman who helped raise me, a woman who sacrificed again and again for me, a woman who loves me as much as she loves anything in this world, but a woman who once confessed her fear of black men who passed by her on the street, and who on more than one occasion has uttered racial or ethnic stereotypes that made me cringe.

These people are a part of me. And they are a part of America, this country that I love.

Some will see this as an attempt to justify or excuse comments that are simply inexcusable. I can assure you it is not. I suppose the politically safe thing would be to move on from this episode and just hope that it fades into the woodwork. We can dismiss Reverend Wright as a crank or a demagogue, just as some have dismissed Geraldine Ferraro, in the aftermath of her recent statements, as harboring some deep-seated racial bias.

But race is an issue that I believe this nation cannot afford to ignore right now. We would be making the same mistake that Reverend Wright made in his offending sermons about America—to simplify and stereotype and amplify the negative to the point that it distorts reality.

The fact is that the comments that have been made and the issues that have surfaced over the last few weeks reflect the complexities of race in this country that we've never really worked through—a part of our union that we have yet to perfect. And if we walk away now, if we simply retreat into our respective corners, we will never be able to come together and solve challenges like health care, or education, or the need to find good jobs for every American.

Understanding this reality requires a reminder of how we arrived at this point. As William Faulkner once wrote, "The past isn't dead and buried. In fact, it isn't even past." We do not need to recite here the history of racial injustice in this country. But we do need to remind ourselves that so many of the disparities that exist in the African American community today can be directly traced to inequalities passed on from an earlier generation that suffered under the brutal legacy of slavery and Jim Crow.

Segregated schools were, and are, inferior schools; we still haven't fixed them, fifty years after *Brown v. Board of Education*, and the inferior education they provided, then and now, helps explain the pervasive achievement gap between today's black and white students.

Legalized discrimination—where blacks were prevented, often through violence, from owning property, or loans were not granted to African American business owners, or black homeowners could not access FHA mortgages, or blacks were excluded from unions, or the police force, or fire departments—meant that black families could not amass any meaningful wealth to bequeath to future generations. That history helps explain the wealth and income gap between black and white, and the concentrated pockets of poverty that persists in so many of today's urban and rural communities.

A lack of economic opportunity among black men, and the shame and frustration that came from not being able to provide for one's family, contributed to the erosion of black families—a problem that welfare policies for many years may have worsened. And the lack of basic services in so many urban black neighborhoods—parks for kids to play in, police walking the beat, regular garbage pick-up and building code enforcement—all helped create a cycle of violence, blight and neglect that continue to haunt us.

This is the reality in which Reverend Wright and other African Americans of his generation grew up. They came of age in the late fifties and early sixties, a time when segregation was still the law of the land and opportunity was systematically constricted. What's remarkable is not how many failed in the face of discrimination, but rather how many men and women overcame the odds; how many were able to make a way out of no way for those like me who would come after them.

But for all those who scratched and clawed their way to get a piece of the American Dream, there were many who didn't make it—those who were ultimately defeated, in one way or another, by discrimination. That legacy of defeat was passed on to future generations—those young men and increasingly young women who we see standing on street corners or languishing in our prisons, without hope or prospects for the future. Even for those blacks who did make it, questions of race, and racism, continue to define their worldview in fundamental ways. For the men and women of Reverend Wright's generation, the memories of humiliation and doubt and fear have not gone away; nor has the anger and the bitterness of those years. That anger may not get expressed in public, in front of white co-workers or white friends. But it does find voice in the barbershop or around the kitchen table. At times, that anger is exploited by politicians, to gin up votes along racial lines, or to make up for a politician's own failings.

And occasionally it finds voice in the church on Sunday morning, in the pulpit and in the pews. The fact that so many people are surprised to hear that anger in some of Reverend Wright's sermons simply reminds us of the old truism that the most segregated hour in American life occurs on Sunday morning. That anger is not always productive; indeed, all too often it distracts attention from solving real problems; it keeps us from squarely facing our own complicity in our condition, and prevents the African American community from forging the alliances it needs to bring about real change. But the anger is real; it is powerful; and to simply wish it away, to condemn it without understanding its roots, only serves to widen the chasm of misunderstanding that exists between the races.

In fact, a similar anger exists within segments of the white community. Most working- and middle-class white Americans don't feel that they have been particularly privileged by their race. Their experience is the immigrant experience—as far as they're concerned, no one's handed them anything, they've built it from scratch. They've worked hard all their lives, many times only to see their jobs shipped overseas or their pension dumped after a lifetime of labor. They are anxious about their futures, and feel their dreams slipping away; in an era of stagnant wages and global competition, opportunity comes to be seen as a zero sum game, in which your dreams come at my expense. So when they are told to bus their children to a school across town; when they hear that an African American is getting an advantage in landing a good job or a spot in a good college because of an injustice that they themselves never committed; when they're told that their fears about crime in urban neighborhoods are somehow prejudiced, resentment builds over time.

Like the anger within the black community, these resentments aren't always expressed in polite company. But they have helped shape the political landscape for at least a generation. Anger over welfare and affirmative action helped forge the Reagan Coalition. Politicians routinely exploited fears of crime for their own electoral ends. Talk show hosts and conservative commentators built entire careers unmasking bogus claims of racism while dismissing legitimate discussions of racial injustice and inequality as mere political correctness or reverse racism.

Just as black anger often proved counterproductive, so have these white resentments distracted attention from the real culprits of the middle class squeeze—a corporate culture rife with inside dealing, questionable accounting practices, and short-term greed; a Washington dominated by lobbyists and special interests; economic policies that favor the few over the many. And yet, to wish away the resentments of white Americans, to label them as misguided or even racist, without recognizing they are grounded in legitimate concerns—this too widens the racial divide, and blocks the path to understanding.

This is where we are right now. It's a racial stalemate we've been stuck in for years. Contrary to the claims of some of my critics, black and white, I have never been so naïve as to believe that we can get beyond our racial divisions in a single election cycle, or with a single candidacy—particularly a candidacy as imperfect as my own.

But I have asserted a firm conviction—a conviction rooted in my faith in God and my faith in the American people—that working together we can move beyond some of our old racial wounds, and that in fact we have no choice if we are to continue on the path of a more perfect union.

For the African American community, that path means embracing the burdens of our past without becoming victims of our past. It means continuing to insist on a full measure of justice in every aspect of American life. But it also means binding our particular grievances—for better health care, and better schools, and better jobs—to the larger aspirations of all Americans—the white woman struggling to break the glass ceiling, the white man who's been laid off, the immigrant trying to feed his family. And it means taking full responsibility for [our] own lives—by demanding more from our fathers, and spending more time with our children, and reading to them, and teaching them that while they may face challenges and discrimination in their own lives, they must never succumb to despair or cynicism; they must always believe that they can write their own destiny.

Ironically, this quintessentially American—and yes, conservative—notion of self-help found frequent expression in Reverend Wright's sermons. But what my former pastor too often failed to understand is that embarking on a program of self-help also requires a belief that society can change.

The profound mistake of Reverend Wright's sermons is not that he spoke about racism in our society. It's that he spoke as if our society was static; as if no progress has been made; as if this country—a country that has made it possible for one of his own members to run for the highest office in the land and build a coalition of white and black, Latino and Asian, rich and poor, young and old—is still irrevocably bound to a tragic past. But what we know—what we have seen—is that America can change. That is the true genius of this nation. What we have already achieved gives us hope—the audacity to hope—for what we can and must achieve tomorrow.

In the white community, the path to a more perfect union means acknowledging that what ails the African American community does not just exist in the minds of black people; that the legacy of discrimination—and current incidents of discrimination, while less overt than in the past—are real and must be addressed. Not just with words, but with deeds—by investing in our schools and our communities; by enforcing our civil rights laws and ensuring fairness in our criminal justice system; by providing this generation with ladders of opportunity that were unavailable for previous generations. It requires all Americans to realize that your dreams do not have to come at the expense of my dreams; that investing in the health, welfare, and education of black and brown and white children will ultimately help all of America prosper.

In the end, then, what is called for is nothing more, and nothing less, than what all the world's great religions demand—that we do unto others as we would have them do unto us. Let us be our brother's keeper, Scripture tells us. Let us be our sister's keeper. Let us find that common stake we all have in one another, and let our politics reflect that spirit as well.

For we have a choice in this country. We can accept a politics that breeds division, and conflict, and cynicism. We can tackle race only as spectacle—as we did in the OJ trial—or in the wake of tragedy, as we did in the aftermath of Katrina—or as fodder for the nightly news. We can play Reverend Wright's sermons on every channel, every day and talk about them from now until the election, and make the only question in this campaign whether or not the American people think that I somehow believe or sympathize with his most offensive words. We can pounce on some gaffe by a Hillary supporter as evidence that she's playing the race card, or we can speculate on whether white men will all flock to John McCain in the general election regardless of his policies.

We can do that.

But if we do, I can tell you that in the next election, we'll be talking about some other distraction. And then another one. And then another one. And nothing will change.

That is one option. Or, at this moment, in this election, we can come together and say, "Not this time." This time we want to talk about the crumbling schools that are stealing the future of black children and white children and Asian children and Hispanic children and Native American children. This time we want to reject the cynicism that tells us that these kids can't learn; that those kids who don't look like us are somebody else's problem. The children of America are not those kids, they are our kids, and we will not let them fall behind in a twenty-first-century economy. Not this time.

This time we want to talk about how the lines in the Emergency Room are filled with whites and blacks and Hispanics who do not have health care; who don't have the power on their own to overcome the special interests in Washington, but who can take them on if we do it together.

This time we want to talk about the shuttered mills that once provided a decent life for men and women of every race, and the homes for sale that once belonged to Americans from every religion, every region, every walk of life. This time we want to talk about the fact that the real problem is not that someone who doesn't look like you might take your job; it's that the corporation you work for will ship it overseas for nothing more than a profit.

This time we want to talk about the men and women of every color and creed who serve together, and fight together, and bleed together under the same proud flag. We want to talk about how to bring them home from a war that never should've been authorized and never should've been waged, and we want to talk about how we'll show our patriotism by caring for them, and their families, and giving them the benefits they have earned.

I would not be running for President if I didn't believe with all my heart that this is what the vast majority of Americans want for this country. This union may never be perfect, but generation after generation has shown that it can always be perfected. And today, whenever I find myself feeling doubtful or cynical about this possibility, what gives me the most hope is the next generation—the young people whose attitudes and beliefs and openness to change have already made history in this election.

There is one story in particular that I'd like to leave you with today—a story I told when I had the great honor of speaking on Dr. King's birthday at his home church, Ebenezer Baptist, in Atlanta.

There is a young, twenty-three-year-old white woman named Ashley Baia who organized for our campaign in Florence, South Carolina. She had been working to organize a mostly African American community since the beginning of this campaign, and one day she was at a roundtable discussion where everyone went around telling their story and why they were there.

And Ashley said that when she was nine years old, her mother got cancer. And because she had to miss days of work, she was let go and lost her health care. They had to file for bankruptcy, and that's when Ashley decided that she had to do something to help her mom.

She knew that food was one of their most expensive costs, and so Ashley convinced her mother that what she really liked and really wanted to eat more than anything else was mustard and relish sandwiches. Because that was the cheapest way to eat.

She did this for a year until her mom got better, and she told everyone at the roundtable that the reason she joined our campaign was so that she could help the millions of other children in the country who want and need to help their parents too.

Now Ashley might have made a different choice. Perhaps somebody told her along the way that the source of her mother's problems were blacks who were on welfare and too lazy to work, or Hispanics who were coming into the country illegally. But she didn't. She sought out allies in her fight against injustice.

Anyway, Ashley finishes her story and then goes around the room and asks everyone else why they're supporting the campaign. They all have different stories and reasons. Many bring up a specific issue. And finally they come to this elderly black man who's been sitting there quietly the entire time. And Ashley asks him why he's there. And he does not bring up a specific issue. He does not say health care or the economy. He does not say education or the war. He does not say that he was there because of Barack Obama. He simply says to everyone in the room, "I am here because of Ashley."

"I'm here because of Ashley." By itself, that single moment of recognition between that young white girl and that old black man is not enough. It is not enough to give health care to the sick, or jobs to the jobless, or education to our children.

But it is where we start. It is where our union grows stronger. And as so many generations have come to realize over the course of the 221 years since a band of patriots signed that document in Philadelphia, that is where the perfection begins.

Acceptance Speech

DEMOCRATIC NATIONAL CONVENTION
DENVER, COLORADO
THURSDAY, AUGUST 28, 2008

TO CHAIRMAN DEAN and my great friend Dick Durbin; and to all my fellow citizens of this great nation. With profound gratitude and great humility, I accept your nomination for the presidency of the United States.

Let me express my thanks to the historic slate of candidates who accompanied me on this journey, and especially the one who traveled the farthest—a champion for working Americans and an inspiration to my daughters and to yours—Hillary Rodham Clinton. To President Clinton, who last night made the case for change as only he can make it; to Ted Kennedy, who embodies the spirit of service; and to the next Vice President of the United States, Joe Biden, I thank you. I am grateful to finish this journey with one of the finest statesmen of our time, a man at ease with everyone from world leaders to the conductors on the Amtrak train he still takes home every night.

To the love of my life, our next First Lady, Michelle Obama, and to Sasha and Malia—I love you so much, and I'm so proud of all of you.

Four years ago, I stood before you and told you my story—of the brief union between a young man from Kenya and a young woman from Kansas who weren't well-off or well-known, but shared a belief that in America, their son could achieve whatever he put his mind to.

It is that promise that has always set this country apart—

that through hard work and sacrifice, each of us can pursue our individual dreams but still come together as one American family, to ensure that the next generation can pursue their dreams as well.

That's why I stand here tonight. Because for 232 years, at each moment when that promise was in jeopardy, ordinary men and women—students and soldiers, farmers and teachers, nurses and janitors—found the courage to keep it alive.

We meet at one of those defining moments—a moment when our nation is at war, our economy is in turmoil, and the American promise has been threatened once more.

Tonight, more Americans are out of work and more are working harder for less. More of you have lost your homes and even more are watching your home values plummet. More of you have cars you can't afford to drive, credit card bills you can't afford to pay, and tuition that's beyond your reach.

These challenges are not all of government's making. But the failure to respond is a direct result of a broken politics in Washington and the failed policies of George W. Bush.

America, we are better than these last eight years. We are a better country than this.

This country is more decent than one where a woman in Ohio, on the brink of retirement, finds herself one illness away from disaster after a lifetime of hard work.

This country is more generous than one where a man in Indiana has to pack up the equipment he's worked on for twenty years and watch it shipped off to China, and then chokes up as he explains how he felt like a failure when he went home to tell his family the news.

We are more compassionate than a government that lets veterans sleep on our streets and families slide into poverty; that sits on its hands while a major American city drowns before our eyes.

Tonight, I say to the American people, to Democrats and Republicans and Independents across this great land—enough! This moment—this election—is our chance to keep, in the twenty-first century, the American promise alive. Because next week, in Minnesota, the same party that brought you two terms of George Bush and Dick Cheney will ask this country for a third. And we are here because we love this country too much to let the next four years look like the last eight. On November 4th, we must stand up and say: "Eight is enough."

Now let there be no doubt. The Republican nominee, John McCain, has worn the uniform of our country with bravery and distinction, and for that we owe him our gratitude and respect. And next week, we'll also hear about those occasions when he's broken with his party as evidence that he can deliver the change that we need.

But the record's clear: John McCain has voted with George Bush ninety percent of the time. Senator McCain likes to talk about judgment, but really, what does it say about your judgment when you think George Bush has been right more than ninety percent of the time? I don't know about you, but I'm not ready to take a ten percent chance on change.

The truth is, on issue after issue that would make a difference in your lives—on health care and education and the economy—Senator McCain has been anything but independent. He said that our economy has made "great progress" under this President. He said that the fundamentals of the economy are strong. And when one of his chief advisors—the man who wrote his economic plan—was talking about the anxiety Americans are feeling, he said that we were just suffering from a "mental recession," and that we've become, and I quote, "a nation of whiners." A nation of whiners? Tell that to the proud auto workers at a Michigan plant who, after they found out it was closing, kept showing up every day and working as hard as ever, because they knew there were people who counted on the brakes that they made. Tell that to the military families who shoulder their burdens silently as they watch their loved ones leave for their third or fourth or fifth tour of duty. These are not whiners. They work hard and give back and keep going without complaint. These are the Americans that I know.

Now, I don't believe that Senator McCain doesn't care what's going on in the lives of Americans. I just think he doesn't know. Why else would he define middle-class as someone making under $5 million a year? How else could he propose hundreds of billions in tax breaks for big corporations and oil companies but not one penny of tax relief to more than 100 million Americans? How else could he offer a health care plan that would actually tax people's benefits, or an education plan that would do nothing to help families pay for college, or a plan that would privatize Social Security and gamble your retirement?

It's not because John McCain doesn't care. It's because John McCain doesn't get it.

For over two decades, he's subscribed to that old, discredited Republican philosophy—give more and more to those with the most and hope that prosperity trickles down to everyone else. In Washington, they call this the Ownership Society, but what it really means is—you're on your own. Out of work? Tough luck. No health care? The market will fix it. Born into poverty? Pull yourself up by your own bootstraps—even if you don't have boots. You're on your own.

Well it's time for them to own their failure. It's time for us to change America.

You see, we Democrats have a very different measure of what constitutes progress in this country.

We measure progress by how many people can find a job that pays the mortgage; whether you can put a little extra money away at the end of each month so you can someday watch your child receive her college diploma. We measure progress in the 23 million new jobs that were created when Bill Clinton was President—when the average American family saw its income go up $7,500 instead of down $2,000 like it has under George Bush.

We measure the strength of our economy not by the number of billionaires we have or the profits of the Fortune 500, but by whether someone with a good idea can take a risk and start a new business, or whether the waitress who lives on tips can take a day off to look after a sick kid without losing her job—an economy that honors the dignity of work.

The fundamentals we use to measure economic strength are whether we are living up to that fundamental promise that has made this country great—a promise that is the only reason I am standing here tonight.

Because in the faces of those young veterans who come back from Iraq and Afghanistan, I see my grandfather, who signed up after Pearl Harbor, marched in Patton's Army, and was rewarded by a grateful nation with the chance to go to college on the GI Bill.

In the face of that young student who sleeps just three hours before working the night shift, I think about my mom, who raised my sister and me on her own while she worked and earned her degree; who once turned to food stamps but was still able to send us to the best schools in the country with the help of student loans and scholarships.

When I listen to another worker tell me that his factory has shut down, I remember all those men and women on the South Side of Chicago who I stood by and fought for two decades ago after the local steel plant closed.

And when I hear a woman talk about the difficulties of starting her own business, I think about my grandmother, who worked her way up from the secretarial pool to middle-management, despite years of being passed over for promotions because she was a woman. She's the one who taught me about hard work. She's the one who put off buying a new car or a new dress for herself so that I could have a better life. She poured everything she had into me. And although she can no longer travel, I know that she's watching tonight, and that tonight is her night as well.

I don't know what kind of lives John McCain thinks that celebrities lead, but this has been mine. These are my heroes. Theirs are the stories that shaped me. And it is on their behalf that I intend to win this election and keep our promise alive as President of the United States.

What is that promise?

It's a promise that says each of us has the freedom to make of our own lives what we will, but that we also have the obligation to treat each other with dignity and respect.

It's a promise that says the market should reward drive and innovation and generate growth, but that businesses should live up to their responsibilities to create American jobs, look out for American workers, and play by the rules of the road.

Ours is a promise that says government cannot solve all our problems, but what it should do is that which we cannot do for ourselves—protect us from harm and provide every child a decent education; keep our water clean and our toys safe; invest in new schools and new roads and new science and technology.

Our government should work for us, not against us. It should help us, not hurt us. It should ensure opportunity not just for those with the most money and influence, but for every American who's willing to work.

That's the promise of America—the idea that we are responsible for ourselves, but that we also rise or fall as one nation; the fundamental belief that I am my brother's keeper; I am my sister's keeper.

That's the promise we need to keep. That's the change we need right now. So let me spell out exactly what that change would mean if I am President.

Change means a tax code that doesn't reward the lobbyists who wrote it, but the American workers and small businesses who deserve it.

Unlike John McCain, I will stop giving tax breaks to corporations that ship jobs overseas, and I will start giving them to companies that create good jobs right here in America.

I will eliminate capital gains taxes for the small businesses and the start-ups that will create the high-wage, high-tech jobs of tomorrow.

I will cut taxes—cut taxes—for 95 percent of all working families. Because in an economy like this, the last thing we should do is raise taxes on the middle-class.

And for the sake of our economy, our security, and the future of our planet, I will set a clear goal as President: in ten years, we will finally end our dependence on oil from the Middle East.

Washington's been talking about our oil addiction for the last thirty years, and John McCain has been there for twenty-six of them. In that time, he's said no to higher fuel-efficiency standards for cars, no to investments in renewable energy, no to renewable fuels. And today, we import triple the amount of oil as the day that Senator McCain took office.

Now is the time to end this addiction, and to understand that drilling is a stop-gap measure, not a long-term solution. Not even close.

As President, I will tap our natural gas reserves, invest in clean coal technology, and find ways to safely harness nuclear power. I'll help our auto companies re-tool, so that the fuel-efficient cars of the future are built right here in America. I'll make it easier for the American people to afford these new cars. And I'll invest $150 billion over the next decade in affordable, renewable sources of energy—wind power and solar power and the next generation of biofuels; an investment that will lead to new industries and 5 million new jobs that pay well and can't ever be outsourced.

America, now is not the time for small plans.

Now is the time to finally meet our moral obligation to provide every child a world-class education, because it will take nothing less to compete in the global economy. Michelle and I are only here tonight because we were given a chance at an education. And I will not settle for an America where some kids don't have that chance. I'll invest in early childhood education. I'll recruit an army of new teachers, and pay them higher salaries and give them more support. And in exchange, I'll ask for higher standards and more accountability. And we will keep our promise to every young American—if you commit to serving your community or your country, we will make sure you can afford a college education.

Now is the time to finally keep the promise of affordable, accessible health care for every single American. If you have health care, my plan will lower your premiums. If you don't, you'll be able to get the same kind of coverage that members of Congress give themselves. And as someone who watched my mother argue with insurance companies while she lay in bed dying of cancer, I will make certain those companies stop discriminating against those who are sick and need care the most.

Now is the time to help families with paid sick days and better family leave, because nobody in America should have to choose between keeping their jobs and caring for a sick child or ailing parent.

Now is the time to change our bankruptcy laws, so that your pensions are protected ahead of CEO bonuses; and the time to protect Social Security for future generations.

And now is the time to keep the promise of equal pay for an equal day's work, because I want my daughters to have exactly the same opportunities as your sons.

Now, many of these plans will cost money, which is why I've laid out how I'll pay for every dime—by closing corporate loopholes and tax havens that don't help America grow. But I will also go through the federal budget, line by line, eliminating programs that no longer work and making the ones we do need work better and cost less—because we cannot meet twenty-first century challenges with a twentieth-century bureaucracy.

And Democrats, we must also admit that fulfilling America's promise will require more than just money. It will require a renewed sense of responsibility from each of us to recover what John F. Kennedy called our "intellectual and moral strength." Yes, government must lead on energy independence, but each of us must do our part to make our homes and businesses more efficient. Yes, we must provide more ladders to success for young men who fall into lives of crime and despair. But we must also admit that programs alone can't replace parents; that government can't turn off the television and make a child do her homework; that fathers must take more responsibility for providing the love and guidance their children need.

Individual responsibility and mutual responsibility—that's the essence of America's promise.

And just as we keep our promise to the next generation here at home, so must we keep America's promise abroad. If John McCain wants to have a debate about who has the temperament, and judgment, to serve as the next Commander-in-Chief, that's a debate I'm ready to have.

For while Senator McCain was turning his sights to Iraq just days after 9/11, I stood up and opposed this war, knowing that it would distract us from the real threats we face. When John McCain said we could just "muddle through" in Afghanistan, I argued for more resources and more troops to finish the fight against the terrorists who actually attacked us on 9/11, and made clear that we must take out Osama bin Laden and his lieutenants if we have them in our sights. John McCain likes to say that he'll follow bin Laden to the Gates of Hell—but he won't even go to the cave where he lives.

And today, as my call for a time frame to remove our troops from Iraq has been echoed by the Iraqi government and even the Bush Administration, even after we learned that Iraq has a $79 billion surplus while we're wallowing in deficits, John McCain stands alone in his stubborn refusal to end a misguided war.

That's not the judgment we need. That won't keep America safe. We need a President who can face the threats of the future, not keep grasping at the ideas of the past.

You don't defeat a terrorist network that operates in eighty countries by occupying Iraq. You don't protect Israel and deter Iran just by talking tough in Washington. You can't truly stand up for Georgia when you've strained our oldest alliances. If John McCain wants to follow George Bush with more tough talk and bad strategy, that is his choice—but it is not the change we need.

We are the party of Roosevelt. We are the party of Kennedy. So don't tell me that Democrats won't defend this country. Don't tell me that Democrats won't keep us safe. The Bush-McCain foreign policy has squandered the legacy that generations of Americans—Democrats and Republicans—have built, and we are here to restore that legacy.

As Commander-in-Chief, I will never hesitate to defend this nation, but I will only send our troops into harm's way with a clear mission and a sacred commitment to give them the equipment they need in battle and the care and benefits they deserve when they come home.

I will end this war in Iraq responsibly, and finish the fight against al Qaeda and the Taliban in Afghanistan. I will rebuild our military to meet future conflicts. But I will also renew the tough, direct diplomacy that can prevent Iran from obtaining nuclear weapons and curb Russian aggression. I will build new partnerships to defeat the threats of the twenty-first century: terrorism and nuclear proliferation; poverty and genocide; climate change and disease. And I will restore our moral standing, so that America is once again that last, best hope for all who are called to the cause of freedom, who long for lives of peace, and who yearn for a better future.

These are the policies I will pursue. And in the weeks ahead, I look forward to debating them with John McCain.

But what I will not do is suggest that the Senator takes his positions for political purposes. Because one of the things that we have to change in our politics is the idea that people cannot disagree without challenging each other's character and patriotism.

The times are too serious, the stakes are too high for this same partisan playbook. So let us agree that patriotism has no party. I love this country, and so do you, and so does John McCain. The men and women who serve in our battlefields may be Democrats and Republicans and Independents, but they have fought together and bled together and some died together under the same proud flag. They have not served a Red America or a Blue America—they have served the United States of America.

So I've got news for you, John McCain. We all put our country first.

America, our work will not be easy. The challenges we face require tough choices, and Democrats as well as Republicans will need to cast off the worn-out ideas and politics of the past. For part of what has been lost these past eight years can't just be measured by lost wages or bigger trade deficits. What has also been lost is our sense of common purpose—our sense of higher purpose. And that's what we have to restore.

We may not agree on abortion, but surely we can agree on reducing the number of unwanted pregnancies in this country. The reality of gun ownership may be different for hunters in rural Ohio than for those plagued by gang violence in Cleveland, but don't tell me we can't uphold the Second Amendment while keeping AK-47s out of the hands of criminals. I know there are differences on same-sex marriage, but surely we can agree that our gay and lesbian brothers and sisters deserve to visit the person they love in the hospital and to live lives free of discrimination. Passions fly on immigration, but I don't know anyone who benefits when a mother is separated from her infant child or an employer undercuts American wages by hiring illegal workers. This too is part of America's promise—the promise of a democracy where we can find the strength and grace to bridge divides and unite in common effort.

I know there are those who dismiss such beliefs as happy talk. They claim that our insistence on something larger, something firmer and more honest in our public life is just a Trojan Horse for higher taxes and the abandonment of traditional values. And that's to be expected. Because if you don't have any fresh ideas, then you use stale tactics to scare the voters. If you don't have a record to run on, then you paint your opponent as someone people should run from.

You make a big election about small things.

And you know what—it's worked before. Because it feeds into the cynicism we all have about government. When Washington doesn't work, all its promises seem empty. If your hopes have been dashed again and again, then it's best to stop hoping, and settle for what you already know.

I get it. I realize that I am not the likeliest candidate for this office. I don't fit the typical pedigree, and I haven't spent my career in the halls of Washington.

But I stand before you tonight because all across America something is stirring. What the nay-sayers don't understand is that this election has never been about me. It's been about you.

For eighteen long months, you have stood up, one by one, and said enough to the politics of the past. You understand that in this election, the greatest risk we can take is to try the same old politics with the same old players and expect a different result. You have shown what history teaches us—that at defining moments like this one, the change we need doesn't come from Washington. Change comes to Washington. Change happens because the American people demand it—because they rise up and insist on new ideas and new leadership, a new politics for a new time.

America, this is one of those moments.

I believe that as hard as it will be, the change we need is coming. Because I've seen it. Because I've lived it. I've seen it in Illinois, when we provided health care to more children and moved more families from welfare to work. I've seen it in Washington, when we worked across party lines to open up government and hold lobbyists more accountable, to give better care for our veterans and keep nuclear weapons out of terrorist hands.

And I've seen it in this campaign. In the young people who voted for the first time, and in those who got involved again after a very long time. In the Republicans who never thought they'd pick up a Democratic ballot, but did. I've seen it in the workers who would rather cut their hours back a day than see their friends lose their jobs, in the soldiers who re-enlist after losing a limb, in the good neighbors who take a stranger in when a hurricane strikes and the floodwaters rise.

This country of ours has more wealth than any nation, but that's not what makes us rich. We have the most powerful military on Earth, but that's not what makes us strong. Our universities and our culture are the envy of the world, but that's not what keeps the world coming to our shores.

Instead, it is that American spirit—that American promise—that pushes us forward even when the path is uncertain; that binds us together in spite of our differences; that makes us fix our eye not on what is seen, but what is unseen, that better place around the bend.

That promise is our greatest inheritance. It's a promise I make to my daughters when I tuck them in at night, and a promise that you make to yours—a promise that has led immigrants to cross oceans and pioneers to travel west; a promise that led workers to picket lines, and women to reach for the ballot.

And it is that promise that forty-five years ago today, brought Americans from every corner of this land to stand together on a Mall in Washington, before Lincoln's Memorial, and hear a young preacher from Georgia speak of his dream.

The men and women who gathered there could've heard many things. They could've heard words of anger and discord. They could've been told to succumb to the fear and frustration of so many dreams deferred.

But what the people heard instead—people of every creed and color, from every walk of life—is that in America, our destiny is inextricably linked. That together, our dreams can be one.

"We cannot walk alone," the preacher cried. "And as we walk, we must make the pledge that we shall always march ahead. We cannot turn back."

America, we cannot turn back. Not with so much work to be done. Not with so many children to educate, and so many veterans to care for. Not with an economy to fix and cities to rebuild and farms to save. Not with so many families to protect and so many lives to mend. America, we cannot turn back. We cannot walk alone. At this moment, in this election, we must pledge once more to march into the future. Let us keep that promise—that American promise—and in the words of Scripture hold firmly, without wavering, to the hope that we confess.

Thank you, God Bless you, and God Bless the United States of America.

First Inaugural Address

WASHINGTON, D.C.
TUESDAY, JANUARY 20, 2009

I STAND HERE TODAY humbled by the task before us, grateful for the trust you have bestowed, mindful of the sacrifices borne by our ancestors. I thank President Bush for his service to our nation, as well as the generosity and cooperation he has shown throughout this transition.

Forty-four Americans have now taken the presidential oath. The words have been spoken during rising tides of prosperity and the still waters of peace. Yet, every so often the oath is taken amidst gathering clouds and raging storms. At these moments, America has carried on not simply because of the skill or vision of those in high office, but because We the People have remained faithful to the ideals of our forebearers, and true to our founding documents.

So it has been. So it must be with this generation of Americans.

That we are in the midst of crisis is now well understood. Our nation is at war, against a far-reaching network of violence and hatred. Our economy is badly weakened, a consequence of greed and irresponsibility on the part of some, but also our collective failure to make hard choices and prepare the nation for a new age. Homes have been lost; jobs shed; businesses shuttered. Our health care is too costly; our schools fail too many; and each day brings further evidence that the ways we use energy strengthen our adversaries and threaten our planet.

These are the indicators of crisis, subject to data and statistics. Less measurable but no less profound is a sapping of confidence across our land—a nagging fear that America's decline is inevitable, and that the next generation must lower its sights.

Today I say to you that the challenges we face are real. They are serious and they are many. They will not be met easily or in a short span of time. But know this, America—they will be met.

On this day, we gather because we have chosen hope over fear, unity of purpose over conflict and discord.

On this day, we come to proclaim an end to the petty grievances and false promises, the recriminations and worn out dogmas, that for far too long have strangled our politics.

We remain a young nation, but in the words of Scripture, the time has come to set aside childish things. The time has come to reaffirm our enduring spirit; to choose our better history; to carry forward that precious gift, that noble idea, passed on from generation to generation: the God-given promise that all are equal, all are free, and all deserve a chance to pursue their full measure of happiness.

In reaffirming the greatness of our nation, we understand that greatness is never a given. It must be earned. Our journey has never been one of short-cuts or settling for less. It has not been the path for the faint-hearted—for those who prefer leisure over work, or seek only the pleasures of riches and fame. Rather, it has been the risk-takers, the doers, the makers of things—some celebrated but more often men and women obscure in their labor, who have carried us up the long, rugged path towards prosperity and freedom.

For us, they packed up their few worldly possessions and traveled across oceans in search of a new life.

For us, they toiled in sweatshops and settled the West; endured the lash of the whip and plowed the hard earth.

For us, they fought and died, in places like Concord and Gettysburg; Normandy and Khe Sahn.

Time and again these men and women struggled and sacrificed and worked till their hands were raw so that we might live a better life. They saw America as bigger than the sum of our individual ambitions; greater than all the differences of birth or wealth or faction.

This is the journey we continue today. We remain the most prosperous, powerful nation on Earth. Our workers are no less productive than when this crisis began. Our minds are no less inventive, our goods and services no less needed than they were last week or last month or last year. Our capacity remains undiminished. But our time of standing pat, of protecting narrow interests and putting off unpleasant decisions—that time has surely passed. Starting today, we must pick ourselves up, dust ourselves off, and begin again the work of remaking America.

For everywhere we look, there is work to be done. The state of the economy calls for action, bold and swift, and we will act—not only to create new jobs, but to lay a new foundation for growth. We will build the roads and bridges, the electric grids and digital lines that feed our commerce and bind us together. We will restore science to its rightful place, and wield technology's wonders to raise health care's quality and lower its cost. We will harness the sun and the winds and the soil to fuel our cars and run our factories. And we will transform our schools and colleges and universities to meet the demands of a new age. All this we can do. And all this we will do.

Now, there are some who question the scale of our ambitions—who suggest that our system cannot tolerate too many big plans. Their memories are short. For they have forgotten what this country has already done; what free men and women can achieve when imagination is joined to common purpose, and necessity to courage.

What the cynics fail to understand is that the ground has shifted beneath them—that the stale political arguments that have consumed us for so long no longer apply. The question we ask today is not whether our government is too big or too small, but whether it works—whether it helps families find jobs at a decent wage, care they can afford, a retirement that is dignified. Where the answer is yes, we intend to move forward. Where the answer is no, programs will end. And those of us who manage the public's dollars will be held to account—to spend wisely, reform bad habits, and do our business in the light of day—because only then can we restore the vital trust between a people and their government.

Nor is the question before us whether the market is a force for good or ill. Its power to generate wealth and expand freedom is unmatched, but this crisis has reminded us that without a watchful eye, the market can spin out of control—and that a nation cannot prosper long when it favors only the prosperous. The success of our economy has always depended not just on the size of our Gross Domestic Product, but on the reach of our prosperity; on our ability to extend opportunity to every willing heart—not out of charity, but because it is the surest route to our common good.

As for our common defense, we reject as false the choice between our safety and our ideals. Our Founding Fathers, faced with perils we can scarcely imagine, drafted a charter to assure the rule of law and the rights of man, a charter expanded by the blood of generations. Those ideals still light the world, and we will not give them up for expedience's sake. And so to all other peoples and governments who are watching today, from the grandest capitals to the small village where my father was born: know that America is a friend of each nation and every man, woman, and child who seeks a future of peace and dignity, and that we are ready to lead once more.

Recall that earlier generations faced down fascism and communism not just with missiles and tanks, but with sturdy alliances and enduring convictions. They understood that our power alone cannot protect us, nor does it entitle us to do as we please. Instead, they knew that our power grows through its prudent use; our security emanates from the justness of our cause, the force of our example, the tempering qualities of humility and restraint.

We are the keepers of this legacy. Guided by these principles once more, we can meet those new threats that demand even greater effort—even greater cooperation and understanding between nations. We will begin to responsibly leave Iraq to its people, and forge a hard-earned peace in Afghanistan. With old friends and former foes, we will work tirelessly to lessen the nuclear threat, and roll back the specter of a warming planet. We will not apologize for our way of life, nor will we waver in its defense, and for those who seek to advance their aims by inducing terror and slaughtering innocents, we say to you now that our spirit is stronger and cannot be broken; you cannot outlast us, and we will defeat you.

For we know that our patchwork heritage is a strength, not a weakness. We are a nation of Christians and Muslims, Jews and Hindus and non-believers. We are shaped by every language and culture, drawn from every end of this Earth; and because we have tasted the bitter swill of civil war and segregation, and emerged from that dark chapter stronger and more united, we cannot help but believe that the old hatreds shall someday pass; that the lines of tribe shall soon dissolve; that as the world grows smaller, our common humanity shall reveal itself; and that America must play its role in ushering in a new era of peace.

To the Muslim world, we seek a new way forward, based on mutual interest and mutual respect. To those leaders around the globe who seek to sow conflict, or blame their society's ills on the West, know that your people will judge you on what you can build, not what you destroy. To those who cling to power through corruption and deceit and the silencing of dissent, know that you are on the wrong side of history; but that we will extend a hand if you are willing to unclench your fist.

To the people of poor nations, we pledge to work alongside you to make your farms flourish and let clean waters flow; to nourish starved bodies and feed hungry minds. And to those nations like ours that enjoy relative plenty, we say we can no longer afford indifference to suffering outside our borders; nor can we consume the world's resources without regard to effect. For the world has changed, and we must change with it.

As we consider the road that unfolds before us, we remember with humble gratitude those brave Americans who, at this very hour, patrol far-off deserts and distant mountains. They have something to tell us today, just as the fallen heroes who lie in Arlington whisper through the ages. We honor them not only because they are guardians of our liberty, but because they embody the spirit of service; a willingness to find meaning in something greater than themselves. And yet, at this moment—a moment that will define a generation—it is precisely this spirit that must inhabit us all.

For as much as government can do and must do, it is ultimately the faith and determination of the American people upon which this nation relies. It is the kindness to take in a stranger when the levees break, the selflessness of workers who would rather cut their hours than see a friend lose their job which sees us through our darkest hours. It is the firefighter's courage to storm a stairway filled with smoke, but also a parent's willingness to nurture a child, that finally decides our fate.

Our challenges may be new. The instruments with which we meet them may be new. But those values upon which our success depends—hard work and honesty, courage and fair play, tolerance and curiosity, loyalty and patriotism—these things are old. These things are true. They have been the quiet force of progress throughout our history. What is demanded then is a return to these truths. What is required of us now is a new era of responsibility—a recognition, on the part of every American, that we have duties to ourselves, our nation, and the world, duties that we do not grudgingly accept but rather seize gladly, firm in the knowledge that there is nothing so satisfying to the spirit, so defining of our character, than giving our all to a difficult task.

This is the price and the promise of citizenship.

This is the source of our confidence—the knowledge that God calls on us to shape an uncertain destiny.

This is the meaning of our liberty and our creed—why men and women and children of every race and every faith can join in celebration across this magnificent Mall, and why a man whose father less than sixty years ago might not have been served at a local restaurant can now stand before you to take a most sacred oath.

So let us mark this day with remembrance, of who we are and how far we have traveled. In the year of America's birth, in the coldest of months, a small band of patriots huddled by dying campfires on the shores of an icy river. The capital was abandoned. The enemy was advancing. The snow was stained with blood. At a moment when the outcome of our revolution was most in doubt, the father of our nation ordered these words be read to the people:

"Let it be told to the future world...that in the depth of

winter, when nothing but hope and virtue could survive... that the city and the country, alarmed at one common danger, came forth to meet [it]."

America. In the face of our common dangers, in this winter of our hardship, let us remember these timeless words. With hope and virtue, let us brave once more the icy currents, and endure what storms may come. Let it be said by our children's children that when we were tested we refused to let this journey end, that we did not turn back nor did we falter; and with eyes fixed on the horizon and God's grace upon us, we carried forth that great gift of freedom and delivered it safely to future generations.

Thank you. God bless you. And may God bless the United States of America.

A New Beginning

CAIRO UNIVERSITY
CAIRO, EGYPT
THURSDAY, JUNE 4, 2009

I AM HONORED to be in the timeless city of Cairo, and to be hosted by two remarkable institutions. For over a thousand years, Al-Azhar has stood as a beacon of Islamic learning, and for over a century, Cairo University has been a source of Egypt's advancement. Together, you represent the harmony between tradition and progress. I am grateful for your hospitality, and the hospitality of the people of Egypt. I am also proud to carry with me the goodwill of the American people, and a greeting of peace from Muslim communities in my country: assalaamu alaykum.

We meet at a time of tension between the United States and Muslims around the world—tension rooted in historical forces that go beyond any current policy debate. The relationship between Islam and the West includes centuries of coexistence and cooperation, but also conflict and religious wars. More recently, tension has been fed by colonialism that denied rights and opportunities to many Muslims, and a Cold War in which Muslim-majority countries were too often treated as proxies without regard to their own aspirations. Moreover, the sweeping change brought by modernity and globalization led many Muslims to view the West as hostile to the traditions of Islam.

Violent extremists have exploited these tensions in a small but potent minority of Muslims. The attacks of September 11th, 2001, and the continued efforts of these extremists to engage in violence against civilians has led some in my country to view Islam as inevitably hostile not only to America and Western countries, but also to human rights. This has bred more fear and mistrust.

So long as our relationship is defined by our differences, we will empower those who sow hatred rather than peace, and who promote conflict rather than the cooperation that can help all of our people achieve justice and prosperity. This cycle of suspicion and discord must end.

I have come here to seek a new beginning between the United States and Muslims around the world; one based upon mutual interest and mutual respect; and one based upon the truth that America and Islam are not exclusive, and need not be in competition. Instead, they overlap, and share common principles—principles of justice and progress; tolerance and the dignity of all human beings.

I do so recognizing that change cannot happen overnight. No single speech can eradicate years of mistrust, nor can I answer in the time that I have all the complex questions that brought us to this point. But I am convinced that in order to move forward, we must say openly the things we hold in our hearts, and that too often are said only behind closed doors. There must be a sustained effort to listen to each other; to learn from each other; to respect one another; and to seek common ground. As the Holy Koran tells us, "Be conscious of God and speak always the truth." That is what I will try to do—to speak the truth as best I can, humbled by the task before us, and firm in my belief that the interests we share as human beings are far more powerful than the forces that drive us apart.

Part of this conviction is rooted in my own experience. I am a Christian, but my father came from a Kenyan family that includes generations of Muslims. As a boy, I spent several years in Indonesia and heard the call of the *azaan* at the break of dawn and the fall of dusk. As a young man, I worked in Chicago communities where many found dignity and peace in their Muslim faith.

As a student of history, I also know civilization's debt to Islam. It was Islam—at places like Al-Azhar University—that carried the light of learning through so many centuries, paving the way for Europe's Renaissance and Enlightenment. It was innovation in Muslim communities that developed the order of algebra; our magnetic compass and tools of navigation; our mastery of pens and printing; our understanding of how disease spreads and how it can be healed. Islamic culture has given us majestic arches and soaring spires; timeless poetry and cherished music; elegant calligraphy and places of peaceful contemplation. And throughout history, Islam has demonstrated through words and deeds the possibilities of religious tolerance and racial equality.

I know, too, that Islam has always been a part of America's story. The first nation to recognize my country was Morocco. In signing the Treaty of Tripoli in 1796, our second President John Adams wrote, "The United States has in itself no character of enmity against the laws, religion or tranquility of Muslims." And since our founding, American Muslims have enriched the United States. They have fought in our wars, served in government, stood for civil rights, started businesses, taught at our Universities, excelled in our sports arenas, won Nobel Prizes, built our tallest building, and lit the Olympic Torch. And when the first Muslim-American was recently elected to Congress, he took the oath to defend our Constitution using the same Holy Koran that one of our Founding Fathers—Thomas Jefferson—kept in his personal library.

So I have known Islam on three continents before coming to the region where it was first revealed. That experience guides my conviction that partnership between America and Islam must be based on what Islam is, not what it isn't. And I consider it part of my responsibility as President of the United States to fight against negative stereotypes of Islam wherever they appear.

But that same principle must apply to Muslim perceptions of America. Just as Muslims do not fit a crude stereotype, America is not the crude stereotype of a self-interested empire. The United States has been one of the greatest sources of progress that the world has ever known. We were born out of revolution against an empire. We were founded upon the ideal that all are created equal, and we have shed blood and struggled for centuries to give meaning to those words—within our borders, and around the world. We are shaped by every culture, drawn from every end of the Earth, and dedicated to a simple concept: *E pluribus unum:* "Out of many, one."

Much has been made of the fact that an African-American with the name Barack Hussein Obama could be elected President. But my personal story is not so unique. The dream of opportunity for all people has not come true for everyone in America, but its promise exists for all who come to our shores—that includes nearly seven million American Muslims in our country today who enjoy incomes and education that are higher than average.

Moreover, freedom in America is indivisible from the freedom to practice one's religion. That is why there is a mosque in every state of our union, and over 1,200 mosques within our borders. That is why the U.S. government has gone to court to protect the right of women and girls to wear the hijab, and to punish those who would deny it.

So let there be no doubt: Islam is a part of America. And I believe that America holds within her the truth that regardless of race, religion, or station in life, all of us share common aspirations—to live in peace and security; to get an education and to work with dignity; to love our families, our communities, and our God. These things we share. This is the hope of all humanity.

Of course, recognizing our common humanity is only the beginning of our task. Words alone cannot meet the needs of our people. These needs will be met only if we act boldly in the years ahead; and if we understand that the challenges we face are shared, and our failure to meet them will hurt us all.

For we have learned from recent experience that when a financial system weakens in one country, prosperity is hurt everywhere. When a new flu infects one human being, all are at risk. When one nation pursues a nuclear weapon, the risk of nuclear attack rises for all nations. When violent extremists operate in one stretch of mountains, people are endangered across an ocean. And when innocents in Bosnia and Darfur are slaughtered, that is a stain on our collective conscience. That is what it means to share this world in the twenty-first century. That is the responsibility we have to one another as human beings.

This is a difficult responsibility to embrace. For human history has often been a record of nations and tribes subjugating one another to serve their own interests. Yet in this new age, such attitudes are self-defeating. Given our interdependence, any world order that elevates one nation or group of people over another will inevitably fail. So whatever we think of the past, we must not be prisoners of it. Our problems must be dealt with through partnership; progress must be shared.

That does not mean we should ignore sources of tension. Indeed, it suggests the opposite: we must face these tensions squarely. And so in that spirit, let me speak as clearly and plainly as I can about some specific issues that I believe we must finally confront together.

The first issue that we have to confront is violent extremism in all of its forms.

In Ankara, I made clear that America is not—and never will be—at war with Islam. We will, however, relentlessly confront violent extremists who pose a grave threat to our security. Because we reject the same thing that people of all faiths reject: the killing of innocent men, women, and children. And it is my first duty as President to protect the American people.

The situation in Afghanistan demonstrates America's goals, and our need to work together. Over seven years ago, the United States pursued al Qaeda and the Taliban with broad international support. We did not go by choice, we went because of necessity. I am aware that some question or justify the events of 9/11. But let us be clear: al Qaeda killed nearly 3,000 people on that day. The victims were innocent men, women and children from America and many other nations who had done nothing to harm anybody. And yet al Qaeda chose to ruthlessly murder these people, claimed credit for the attack, and even now states their determination to kill on a massive scale. They have affiliates in many countries and are trying to expand their reach. These are not opinions to be debated; these are facts to be dealt with.

Make no mistake: we do not want to keep our troops in Afghanistan. We seek no military bases there. It is agonizing for America to lose our young men and women. It is costly and politically difficult to continue this conflict. We would gladly bring every single one of our troops home if we could be confident that there were not violent extremists in Afghanistan and Pakistan determined to kill as many Americans as they possibly can. But that is not yet the case.

That's why we're partnering with a coalition of forty-six countries. And despite the costs involved, America's commitment will not weaken. Indeed, none of us should tolerate these extremists. They have killed in many countries. They have killed people of different faiths—more than any other, they have killed Muslims. Their actions are irreconcilable with the rights of human beings, the progress of nations, and with Islam. The Holy Koran teaches that whoever kills an innocent, it is as if he has killed all mankind; and whoever saves a person, it is as if he has saved all mankind. The enduring faith of over a billion people is so much bigger than the narrow hatred of a few. Islam is not part of the problem in combating violent extremism—it is an important part of promoting peace.

We also know that military power alone is not going to solve the problems in Afghanistan and Pakistan. That is why we plan to invest $1.5 billion each year over the next five years to partner with Pakistanis to build schools and hospitals, roads and businesses, and hundreds of millions to help those who have been displaced. And that is why we are providing more than $2.8 billion to help Afghans develop their economy and deliver services that people depend upon.

Let me also address the issue of Iraq. Unlike Afghanistan, Iraq was a war of choice that provoked strong differences in my country and around the world. Although I believe that the Iraqi people are ultimately better off without the tyranny of Saddam Hussein, I also believe that events in Iraq have reminded America of the need to use diplomacy and build international consensus to resolve our problems whenever possible. Indeed, we can recall the words of Thomas Jefferson, who said: "I hope that our wisdom will grow with our power, and teach us that the less we use our power the greater it will be."

Today, America has a dual responsibility: to help Iraq forge a better future—and to leave Iraq to Iraqis. I have made it clear to the Iraqi people that we pursue no bases, and no claim on their territory or resources. Iraq's sovereignty is its own. That is why I ordered the removal of our combat brigades by next August. That is why we will honor our agreement with Iraq's democratically elected government to remove combat troops from Iraqi cities by July, and to remove all our troops from Iraq by 2012. We will help Iraq train its Security Forces and develop its economy. But we will support a secure and united Iraq as a partner, and never as a patron.

And finally, just as America can never tolerate violence by extremists, we must never alter our principles. Nine-eleven was an enormous trauma to our country. The fear and anger that it provoked was understandable, but in some cases, it led us to act contrary to our ideals. We are taking concrete actions to change course. I have unequivocally prohibited the use of torture by the United States, and I have ordered the prison at Guantanamo Bay closed by early next year.

So America will defend itself respectful of the sovereignty of nations and the rule of law. And we will do so in partnership with Muslim communities which are also threatened. The sooner the extremists are isolated and unwelcome in Muslim communities, the sooner we will all be safer.

The second major source of tension that we need to discuss is the situation between Israelis, Palestinians and the Arab world.

America's strong bonds with Israel are well known. This bond is unbreakable. It is based upon cultural and historical ties, and the recognition that the aspiration for a Jewish homeland is rooted in a tragic history that cannot be denied.

Around the world, the Jewish people were persecuted for centuries, and anti-Semitism in Europe culminated in an unprecedented Holocaust. Tomorrow, I will visit Buchenwald, which was part of a network of camps where Jews were enslaved, tortured, shot and gassed to death by the Third Reich. Six million Jews were killed—more than the entire Jewish population of Israel today. Denying that fact is baseless, ignorant, and hateful. Threatening Israel with destruction—or repeating vile stereotypes about Jews—is deeply wrong, and only serves to evoke in the minds of Israelis this most painful of memories while preventing the peace that the people of this region deserve.

On the other hand, it is also undeniable that the Palestinian people—Muslims and Christians—have suffered in pursuit of a homeland. For more than sixty years they have endured the pain of dislocation. Many wait in refugee camps in the West Bank, Gaza, and neighboring lands for a life of peace and security that they have never been able to lead. They endure the daily humiliations—large and small—that come with occupation. So let there be no doubt: the situation for the Palestinian people is intolerable. America will not turn our backs on the legitimate Palestinian aspiration for dignity, opportunity, and a state of their own.

For decades, there has been a stalemate: two peoples with legitimate aspirations, each with a painful history that makes compromise elusive. It is easy to point fingers—for Palestinians to point to the displacement brought by Israel's founding, and for Israelis to point to the constant hostility and attacks throughout its history from within its borders as well as beyond. But if we see this conflict only from one side or the other, then we will be blind to the truth: the only resolution is for the aspirations of both sides to be met through two states, where Israelis and Palestinians each live in peace and security.

That is in Israel's interest, Palestine's interest, America's interest, and the world's interest. That is why I intend to personally pursue this outcome with all the patience that the task requires. The obligations that the parties have agreed to under the Road Map are clear. For peace to come, it is time for them—and all of us—to live up to our responsibilities.

Palestinians must abandon violence. Resistance through violence and killing is wrong and does not succeed. For centuries, black people in America suffered the lash of the whip as slaves and the humiliation of segregation. But it was not violence that won full and equal rights. It was a peaceful and determined insistence upon the ideals at the center of America's founding. This same story can be told by people from South Africa to South Asia; from Eastern Europe to Indonesia. It's a story with a simple truth: that violence is a dead end. It is a sign of neither courage nor power to shoot rockets at sleeping children, or to blow up old women on a bus. That is not how moral authority is claimed; that is how it is surrendered.

Now is the time for Palestinians to focus on what they can build. The Palestinian Authority must develop its capacity to govern, with institutions that serve the needs of its people. Hamas does have support among some Palestinians, but they also have responsibilities. To play a role in fulfilling Palestinian aspirations, and to unify the Palestinian people, Hamas must put an end to violence, recognize past agreements, and recognize Israel's right to exist.

At the same time, Israelis must acknowledge that just as Israel's right to exist cannot be denied, neither can Palestine's. The United States does not accept the legitimacy of continued Israeli settlements. This construction violates previous agreements and undermines efforts to achieve peace. It is time for these settlements to stop.

Israel must also live up to its obligations to ensure that Palestinians can live, and work, and develop their society. And just as it devastates Palestinian families, the continuing humanitarian crisis in Gaza does not serve Israel's security; neither does the continuing lack of opportunity in the West Bank. Progress in the daily lives of the Palestinian people must be part of a road to peace, and Israel must take concrete steps to enable such progress.

Finally, the Arab States must recognize that the Arab Peace Initiative was an important beginning, but not the end of their responsibilities. The Arab-Israeli conflict should no longer be used to distract the people of Arab nations from other problems. Instead, it must be a cause for action to help the Palestinian people develop the institutions that will sustain their state; to recognize Israel's legitimacy; and to choose progress over a self-defeating focus on the past.

America will align our policies with those who pursue peace, and say in public what we say in private to Israelis and Palestinians and Arabs. We cannot impose peace. But privately, many Muslims recognize that Israel will not go away. Likewise, many Israelis recognize the need for a Palestinian state. It is time for us to act on what everyone knows to be true.

Too many tears have flowed. Too much blood has been shed. All of us have a responsibility to work for the day when the mothers of Israelis and Palestinians can see their children grow up without fear; when the Holy Land of three great faiths is the place of peace that God intended it to be; when Jerusalem is a secure and lasting home for Jews and Christians and Muslims, and a place for all of the children of Abraham to mingle peacefully together as in the story of Isra, when Moses, Jesus, and Mohammed (peace be upon them) joined in prayer.

The third source of tension is our shared interest in the rights and responsibilities of nations on nuclear weapons.

This issue has been a source of tension between the United States and the Islamic Republic of Iran. For many years, Iran has defined itself in part by its opposition to my country, and there is indeed a tumultuous history between us. In the middle of the Cold War, the United States played a role in the overthrow of a democratically-elected Iranian government. Since the Islamic Revolution, Iran has played a role in acts of hostage-taking and violence against U.S. troops and civilians. This history is well known. Rather than remain trapped in the past, I have made it clear to Iran's leaders and people that my country is prepared to move forward. The question, now, is not what Iran is against, but rather what future it wants to build.

It will be hard to overcome decades of mistrust, but we will proceed with courage, rectitude and resolve. There will be many issues to discuss between our two countries, and we are willing to move forward without preconditions on the basis of mutual respect. But it is clear to all concerned that when it comes to nuclear weapons, we have reached a decisive point. This is not simply about America's interests. It is about preventing a nuclear arms race in the Middle East that could lead this region and the world down a hugely dangerous path.

I understand those who protest that some countries have weapons that others do not. No single nation should pick and choose which nations hold nuclear weapons. That is why I strongly reaffirmed America's commitment to seek a world in which no nations hold nuclear weapons. And any nation—including Iran—should have the right to access peaceful nuclear power if it complies with its responsibilities under the nuclear Non-Proliferation Treaty. That commitment is at the core of the Treaty, and it must be kept for all who fully abide by it. And I am hopeful that all countries in the region can share in this goal.

The fourth issue that I will address is democracy.

I know there has been controversy about the promotion of democracy in recent years, and much of this controversy is connected to the war in Iraq. So let me be clear: no system of government can or should be imposed upon one nation by any other.

That does not lessen my commitment, however, to governments that reflect the will of the people. Each nation gives life to this principle in its own way, grounded in the traditions of its own people. America does not presume to know what is best for everyone, just as we would not presume to pick the outcome of a peaceful election. But I do have an unyielding belief that all people yearn for certain things: the ability to speak your mind and have a say in how you are governed; confidence in the rule of law and the equal administration of justice; government that is transparent and doesn't steal from the people; the freedom to live as you choose. Those are not just American ideas, they are human rights, and that is why we will support them everywhere.

There is no straight line to realize this promise. But this much is clear: governments that protect these rights are ultimately more stable, successful and secure. Suppressing ideas never succeeds in making them go away. America respects the right of all peaceful and law-abiding voices to be heard around the world, even if we disagree with them. And we will welcome all elected, peaceful governments—provided they govern with respect for all their people.

This last point is important because there are some who advocate for democracy only when they are out of power; once in power, they are ruthless in suppressing the rights of others. No matter where it takes hold, government of the people and by the people sets a single standard for all who hold power: you must maintain your power through consent, not coercion; you must respect the rights of minorities, and participate with a spirit of tolerance and compromise; you must place the interests of your people and the legitimate workings of the political process above your party. Without these ingredients, elections alone do not make true democracy.

The fifth issue that we must address together is religious freedom.

Islam has a proud tradition of tolerance. We see it in the history of Andalusia and Cordoba during the Inquisition. I saw it firsthand as a child in Indonesia, where devout Christians worshiped freely in an overwhelmingly Muslim country. That is the spirit we need today. People in every country should be free to choose and live their faith based upon the persuasion of the mind, heart, and soul. This tolerance is essential for religion to thrive, but it is being challenged in many different ways.

Among some Muslims, there is a disturbing tendency to measure one's own faith by the rejection of another's. The richness of religious diversity must be upheld—whether it is for Maronites in Lebanon or the Copts in Egypt. And fault lines must be closed among Muslims as well, as the divisions between Sunni and Shia have led to tragic violence, particularly in Iraq.

Freedom of religion is central to the ability of peoples to live together. We must always examine the ways in which we protect it. For instance, in the United States, rules on charitable giving have made it harder for Muslims to fulfill their religious obligation. That is why I am committed to working with American Muslims to ensure that they can fulfill *zakat*.

Likewise, it is important for Western countries to avoid impeding Muslim citizens from practicing religion as they see fit—for instance, by dictating what clothes a Muslim woman should wear. We cannot disguise hostility towards any religion behind the pretence of liberalism.

Indeed, faith should bring us together. That is why we are forging service projects in America that bring together Christians, Muslims, and Jews. That is why we welcome efforts like Saudi Arabian King Abdullah's Interfaith dialogue and Turkey's leadership in the Alliance of Civilizations. Around the world, we can turn dialogue into Interfaith service, so bridges between peoples lead to action—whether it is combating malaria in Africa, or providing relief after a natural disaster.

The sixth issue that I want to address is women's rights.

I know there is debate about this issue. I reject the view of some in the West that a woman who chooses to cover her hair is somehow less equal, but I do believe that a woman who is denied an education is denied equality. And it is no coincidence that countries where women are well-educated are far more likely to be prosperous.

Now let me be clear: issues of women's equality are by no means simply an issue for Islam. In Turkey, Pakistan, Bangladesh and Indonesia, we have seen Muslim-majority countries elect a woman to lead. Meanwhile, the struggle for women's equality continues in many aspects of American life, and in countries around the world.

Our daughters can contribute just as much to society as our sons, and our common prosperity will be advanced by allowing all humanity—men and women—to reach their full potential. I do not believe that women must make the same choices as men in order to be equal, and I respect those women who choose to live their lives in traditional roles. But it should be their choice. That is why the United States will partner with any Muslim-majority country to support expanded literacy for girls, and to help young women pursue employment through micro-financing that helps people live their dreams.

Finally, I want to discuss economic development and opportunity.

I know that for many, the face of globalization is contradictory. The Internet and television can bring knowledge and information, but also offensive sexuality and mindless violence. Trade can bring new wealth and opportunities, but also huge disruptions and changing communities. In all nations—including my own—this change can bring fear. Fear that because of modernity we will lose control over our economic choices, our politics, and most importantly our identities—those things we most cherish about our communities, our families, our traditions, and our faith.

But I also know that human progress cannot be denied. There need not be contradiction between development and tradition. Countries like Japan and South Korea grew their economies while maintaining distinct cultures. The same is true for the astonishing progress within Muslim-majority countries from Kuala Lumpur to Dubai. In ancient times and in our times, Muslim communities have been at the forefront of innovation and education.

This is important because no development strategy can be based only upon what comes out of the ground, nor can it be sustained while young people are out of work. Many Gulf States have enjoyed great wealth as a consequence of oil, and some are beginning to focus it on broader development. But all of us must recognize that education and innovation will be the currency of the twenty-first century, and in too many Muslim communities there remains underinvestment in these areas. I am emphasizing such investments within my country. And while America in the past has focused on oil and gas in this part of the world, we now seek a broader engagement.

On education, we will expand exchange programs, and increase scholarships, like the one that brought my father to America, while encouraging more Americans to study in Muslim communities. And we will match promising Muslim students with internships in America; invest in on-line learning for teachers and children around the world; and create a new online network, so a teenager in Kansas can communicate instantly with a teenager in Cairo.

On economic development, we will create a new corps of business volunteers to partner with counterparts in Muslim-majority countries. And I will host a Summit on Entrepreneurship this year to identify how we can deepen ties between business leaders, foundations and social entrepreneurs in the United States and Muslim communities around the world.

On science and technology, we will launch a new fund to support technological development in Muslim-majority countries, and to help transfer ideas to the marketplace so they can create jobs. We will open centers of scientific excellence in Africa, the Middle East and Southeast Asia, and appoint new Science Envoys to collaborate on programs that develop new sources of energy, create green jobs, digitize records, clean water, and grow new crops. And today I am announcing a new global effort with the Organization of the Islamic Conference to eradicate polio. And we will also expand partnerships with Muslim communities to promote child and maternal health.

All these things must be done in partnership. Americans are ready to join with citizens and governments, community organizations, religious leaders, and businesses in Muslim communities around the world to help our people pursue a better life.

The issues that I have described will not be easy to address. But we have a responsibility to join together on behalf of the world we seek—a world where extremists no longer threaten our people, and American troops have come home; a world where Israelis and Palestinians are each secure in a state of their own, and nuclear energy is used for peaceful purposes; a world where governments serve their citizens, and the rights of all God's children are respected. Those are mutual interests. That is the world we seek. But we can only achieve it together.

I know there are many—Muslim and non-Muslim—who question whether we can forge this new beginning. Some are eager to stoke the flames of division, and to stand in the way of progress. Some suggest that it isn't worth the effort—that we are fated to disagree, and civilizations are doomed to clash. Many more are simply skeptical that real change can occur. There is so much fear, so much mistrust. But if we choose to be bound by the past, we will never move forward. And I want to particularly say this to young people of every faith, in every country — you, more than anyone, have the ability to remake this world.

All of us share this world for but a brief moment in time. The question is whether we spend that time focused on what pushes us apart, or whether we commit ourselves to an effort—a sustained effort—to find common ground, to focus on the future we seek for our children, and to respect the dignity of all human beings.

It is easier to start wars than to end them. It is easier to blame others than to look inward; to see what is different about someone than to find the things we share. But we should choose the right path, not just the easy path. There is also one rule that lies at the heart of every religion—that we do unto others as we would have them do unto us. This truth transcends nations and peoples—a belief that isn't new; that isn't black or white or brown; that isn't Christian, or Muslim or Jew. It's a belief that pulsed in the cradle of civilization, and that still beats in the heart of billions. It's a faith in other people, and it's what brought me here today.

We have the power to make the world we seek, but only if we have the courage to make a new beginning, keeping in mind what has been written.

The Holy Koran tells us, "O mankind! We have created you male and a female; and we have made you into nations and tribes so that you may know one another."

The Talmud tells us: "The whole of the Torah is for the purpose of promoting peace."

The Holy Bible tells us, "Blessed are the peacemakers, for they shall be called sons of God."

The people of the world can live together in peace. We know that is God's vision. Now, that must be our work here on Earth. Thank you. And may God's peace be upon you.

Acceptance of the Nobel Peace Prize

OSLO CITY HALL
OSLO, NORWAY
THURSDAY, DECEMBER 10, 2009

Your Majesties, Your Royal Highnesses, distinguished members of the Norwegian Nobel Committee, citizens of America, and citizens of the world:

I RECEIVE THIS HONOR with deep gratitude and great humility. It is an award that speaks to our highest aspirations—that for all the cruelty and hardship of our world, we are not mere prisoners of fate. Our actions matter, and can bend history in the direction of justice.

And yet I would be remiss if I did not acknowledge the considerable controversy that your generous decision has generated. In part, this is because I am at the beginning, and not the end, of my labors on the world stage. Compared to some of the giants of history who've received this prize—Schweitzer and King; Marshall and Mandela—my accomplishments are slight. And then there are the men and women around the world who have been jailed and beaten in the pursuit of justice; those who toil in humanitarian organizations to relieve suffering; the unrecognized millions whose quiet acts of courage and compassion inspire even the most hardened cynics. I cannot argue with those who find these men and women—some known, some obscure to all but those they help—to be far more deserving of this honor than I.

But perhaps the most profound issue surrounding my receipt of this prize is the fact that I am the Commander-in-Chief of the military of a nation in the midst of two wars. One of these wars is winding down. The other is a conflict that America did not seek; one in which we are joined by forty-two other countries—including Norway—in an effort to defend ourselves and all nations from further attacks.

Still, we are at war, and I'm responsible for the deployment of thousands of young Americans to battle in a distant land. Some will kill, and some will be killed. And so I come here with an acute sense of the costs of armed conflict—filled with difficult questions about the relationship between war and peace, and our effort to replace one with the other.

Now these questions are not new. War, in one form or another, appeared with the first man. At the dawn of history, its morality was not questioned; it was simply a fact, like drought or disease—the manner in which tribes and then civilizations sought power and settled their differences.

And over time, as codes of law sought to control violence within groups, so did philosophers and clerics and statesmen seek to regulate the destructive power of war. The concept of a "just war" emerged, suggesting that war is justified only when certain conditions were met: if it is waged as a last resort or in self-defense; if the force used is proportional; and if, whenever possible, civilians are spared from violence.

Of course, we know that for most of history, this concept of "just war" was rarely observed. The capacity of human beings to think up new ways to kill one another proved inexhaustible, as did our capacity to exempt from mercy those who look different or pray to a different God. Wars between armies gave way to wars between nations—total wars in which the distinction between combatant and civilian became blurred. In the span of thirty years, such carnage would twice engulf this continent. And while it's hard to conceive of a cause more just than the defeat of the Third Reich and the Axis powers, World

War II was a conflict in which the total number of civilians who died exceeded the number of soldiers who perished.

In the wake of such destruction, and with the advent of the nuclear age, it became clear to victor and vanquished alike that the world needed institutions to prevent another world war. And so, a quarter century after the United States Senate rejected the League of Nations—an idea for which Woodrow Wilson received this prize—America led the world in constructing an architecture to keep the peace: a Marshall Plan and a United Nations, mechanisms to govern the waging of war, treaties to protect human rights, prevent genocide, restrict the most dangerous weapons.

In many ways, these efforts succeeded. Yes, terrible wars have been fought, and atrocities committed. But there has been no Third World War. The Cold War ended with jubilant crowds dismantling a wall. Commerce has stitched much of the world together. Billions have been lifted from poverty. The ideals of liberty and self-determination, equality and the rule of law have haltingly advanced. We are the heirs of the fortitude and foresight of generations past, and it is a legacy for which my own country is rightfully proud.

And yet, a decade into a new century, this old architecture is buckling under the weight of new threats. The world may no longer shudder at the prospect of war between two nuclear superpowers, but proliferation may increase the risk of catastrophe. Terrorism has long been a tactic, but modern technology allows a few small men with outsized rage to murder innocents on a horrific scale.

Moreover, wars between nations have increasingly given way to wars within nations. The resurgence of ethnic or sectarian conflicts; the growth of secessionist movements, insurgencies, and failed states—all these things have increasingly trapped civilians in unending chaos. In today's wars, many more civilians are killed than soldiers; the seeds of future conflict are sown, economies are wrecked, civil societies torn asunder, refugees amassed, children scarred.

I do not bring with me today a definitive solution to the problems of war. What I do know is that meeting these challenges will require the same vision, hard work, and persistence of those men and women who acted so boldly decades ago. And it will require us to think in new ways about the notions of just war and the imperatives of a just peace.

We must begin by acknowledging the hard truth: We will not eradicate violent conflict in our lifetimes. There will be times when nations—acting individually or in concert—will find the use of force not only necessary but morally justified.

I make this statement mindful of what Martin Luther King Jr. said in this same ceremony years ago: "Violence never brings permanent peace. It solves no social problem: it merely creates new and more complicated ones." As someone who stands here as a direct consequence of Dr. King's life work, I am living testimony to the moral force of non-violence. I know there's nothing weak—nothing passive—nothing naïve—in the creed and lives of Gandhi and King.

But as a head of state sworn to protect and defend my nation, I cannot be guided by their examples alone. I face the world as it is, and cannot stand idle in the face of threats to the American people. For make no mistake: Evil does exist in the world. A non-violent movement could not have halted Hitler's armies. Negotiations cannot convince al Qaeda's leaders to lay down their arms. To say that force may sometimes be necessary is not a call to cynicism—it is a recognition of history; the imperfections of man and the limits of reason.

I raise this point, I begin with this point because in many countries there is a deep ambivalence about military action today, no matter what the cause. And at times, this is joined by a reflexive suspicion of America, the world's sole military superpower.

But the world must remember that it was not simply international institutions—not just treaties and declarations—that brought stability to a post–World War II world. Whatever mistakes we have made, the plain fact is this: The United States of America has helped underwrite global security for more than six decades with the blood of our citizens and the strength of our arms. The service and sacrifice of our men and women in uniform has promoted peace and prosperity from Germany to Korea, and enabled democracy to take hold in places like the Balkans. We have borne this burden not because we seek to impose our will. We have done so out of enlightened self-interest—because we seek a better future for our children and grandchildren, and we believe that their lives will be better if others' children and grandchildren can live in freedom and prosperity.

So yes, the instruments of war do have a role to play in preserving the peace. And yet this truth must coexist with another—that no matter how justified, war promises human tragedy. The soldier's courage and sacrifice is full of glory, expressing devotion to country, to cause, to comrades in arms. But war itself is never glorious, and we must never trumpet it as such.

So part of our challenge is reconciling these two seemingly irreconcilable truths—that war is sometimes necessary, and war at some level is an expression of human folly. Concretely, we must direct our effort to the task that President Kennedy called for long ago. "Let us focus," he said, "on a more practical, more attainable peace, based not on a sudden revolution in human nature but on a gradual evolution in human institutions." A gradual evolution of human institutions.

What might this evolution look like? What might these practical steps be?

To begin with, I believe that all nations—strong and weak alike—must adhere to standards that govern the use of force. I—like any head of state—reserve the right to act unilaterally if necessary to defend my nation. Nevertheless, I am convinced that adhering to standards, international standards, strengthens those who do, and isolates and weakens those who don't.

The world rallied around America after the 9/11 attacks, and continues to support our efforts in Afghanistan, because of the horror of those senseless attacks and the recognized principle of self-defense. Likewise, the world recognized the need to confront Saddam Hussein when he invaded Kuwait—a consensus that sent a clear message to all about the cost of aggression.

Furthermore, America—in fact, no nation—can insist that others follow the rules of the road if we refuse to follow them ourselves. For when we don't, our actions appear arbitrary and undercut the legitimacy of future interventions, no matter how justified.

And this becomes particularly important when the purpose of military action extends beyond self-defense or the defense of one nation against an aggressor. More and more, we all confront difficult questions about how to prevent the slaughter of civilians by their own government, or to stop a civil war whose violence and suffering can engulf an entire region.

I believe that force can be justified on humanitarian grounds, as it was in the Balkans, or in other places that have been scarred by war. Inaction tears at our conscience and can lead to more costly intervention later. That's why all responsible nations must embrace the role that militaries with a clear mandate can play to keep the peace.

America's commitment to global security will never waver. But in a world in which threats are more diffuse, and missions more complex, America cannot act alone. America alone cannot secure the peace. This is true in Afghanistan. This is true in failed states like Somalia, where terrorism and piracy is joined by famine and human suffering. And sadly, it will continue to be true in unstable regions for years to come.

The leaders and soldiers of NATO countries, and other friends and allies, demonstrate this truth through the capacity and courage they've shown in Afghanistan. But in many countries, there is a disconnect between the efforts of those who serve and the ambivalence of the broader public. I understand why war is not popular, but I also know this: The belief that peace is desirable is rarely enough to achieve it. Peace requires responsibility. Peace entails sacrifice. That's why NATO continues to be indispensable. That's why we must strengthen U.N. and regional peacekeeping, and not leave the task to a few countries. That's why we honor those who return home from peacekeeping and training abroad to Oslo and Rome; to Ottawa and Sydney; to Dhaka and Kigali—we honor them not as makers of war, but of wagers—but as wagers of peace.

Let me make one final point about the use of force. Even as we make difficult decisions about going to war, we must also think clearly about how we fight it. The Nobel Committee recognized this truth in awarding its first prize for peace to Henry Dunant—the founder of the Red Cross, and a driving force behind the Geneva Conventions.

Where force is necessary, we have a moral and strategic interest in binding ourselves to certain rules of conduct. And even as we confront a vicious adversary that abides by no rules, I believe the United States of America must remain a standard bearer in the conduct of war. That is what makes us different from those whom we fight. That is a source of our strength. That is why I prohibited torture. That is why I ordered the prison at Guantanamo Bay closed. And that is why I have reaffirmed America's commitment to abide by the Geneva

Conventions. We lose ourselves when we compromise the very ideals that we fight to defend. And we honor—we honor those ideals by upholding them not when it's easy, but when it is hard.

I have spoken at some length to the question that must weigh on our minds and our hearts as we choose to wage war. But let me now turn to our effort to avoid such tragic choices, and speak of three ways that we can build a just and lasting peace.

First, in dealing with those nations that break rules and laws, I believe that we must develop alternatives to violence that are tough enough to actually change behavior—for if we want a lasting peace, then the words of the international community must mean something. Those regimes that break the rules must be held accountable. Sanctions must exact a real price. Intransigence must be met with increased pressure—and such pressure exists only when the world stands together as one.

One urgent example is the effort to prevent the spread of nuclear weapons, and to seek a world without them. In the middle of the last century, nations agreed to be bound by a treaty whose bargain is clear: All will have access to peaceful nuclear power; those without nuclear weapons will forsake them; and those with nuclear weapons will work towards disarmament. I am committed to upholding this treaty. It is a centerpiece of my foreign policy. And I'm working with President Medvedev to reduce America and Russia's nuclear stockpiles.

But it is also incumbent upon all of us to insist that nations like Iran and North Korea do not game the system. Those who claim to respect international law cannot avert their eyes when those laws are flouted. Those who care for their own security cannot ignore the danger of an arms race in the Middle East or East Asia. Those who seek peace cannot stand idly by as nations arm themselves for nuclear war.

The same principle applies to those who violate international laws by brutalizing their own people. When there is genocide in Darfur, systematic rape in Congo, repression in Burma—there must be consequences. Yes, there will be engagement; yes, there will be diplomacy—but there must be consequences when those things fail. And the closer we stand together, the less likely we will be faced with the choice between armed intervention and complicity in oppression.

This brings me to a second point—the nature of the peace that we seek. For peace is not merely the absence of visible conflict. Only a just peace based on the inherent rights and dignity of every individual can truly be lasting.

It was this insight that drove drafters of the Universal Declaration of Human Rights after the Second World War. In the wake of devastation, they recognized that if human rights are not protected, peace is a hollow promise.

And yet too often, these words are ignored. For some countries, the failure to uphold human rights is excused by the false suggestion that these are somehow Western principles, foreign to local cultures or stages of a nation's development. And within America, there has long been a tension between those who describe themselves as realists or idealists—a tension that suggests a stark choice between the narrow pursuit of interests or an endless campaign to impose our values around the world.

I reject these choices. I believe that peace is unstable where citizens are denied the right to speak freely or worship as they please; choose their own leaders or assemble without fear. Pent-up grievances fester, and the suppression of tribal and religious identity can lead to violence. We also know that the opposite is true. Only when Europe became free did it finally find peace. America has never fought a war against a democracy, and our closest friends are governments that protect the rights of their citizens. No matter how callously defined, neither America's interests—nor the world's—are served by the denial of human aspirations.

So even as we respect the unique culture and traditions of different countries, America will always be a voice for those aspirations that are universal. We will bear witness to the quiet dignity of reformers like Aung San Suu Kyi; to the bravery of Zimbabweans who cast their ballots in the face of beatings; to the hundreds of thousands who have marched silently through the streets of Iran. It is telling that the leaders of these governments fear the aspirations of their own people more than the power of any other nation. And it is the responsibility of all free people and free nations to make clear that these movements—these movements of hope and history—they have us on their side.

Let me also say this: The promotion of human rights cannot be about exhortation alone. At times, it must be coupled with painstaking diplomacy. I know that engagement with repressive regimes lacks the satisfying purity of indignation. But I also know that sanctions without outreach—condemnation without discussion—can carry forward only a crippling status quo. No repressive regime can move down a new path unless it has the choice of an open door.

In light of the Cultural Revolution's horrors, Nixon's meeting with Mao appeared inexcusable—and yet it surely helped set China on a path where millions of its citizens have been lifted from poverty and connected to open societies. Pope John Paul's engagement with Poland created space not just for the Catholic Church, but for labor leaders like Lech Walesa. Ronald Reagan's efforts on arms control and embrace of perestroika not only improved relations with the Soviet Union, but empowered dissidents throughout Eastern Europe. There's no simple formula here. But we must try as best we can to balance isolation and engagement, pressure and incentives, so that human rights and dignity are advanced over time.

Third, a just peace includes not only civil and political rights—it must encompass economic security and opportunity. For true peace is not just freedom from fear, but freedom from want.

It is undoubtedly true that development rarely takes root without security; it is also true that security does not exist where human beings do not have access to enough food, or clean water, or the medicine and shelter they need to survive. It does not exist where children can't aspire to a decent education or a job that supports a family. The absence of hope can rot a society from within.

And that's why helping farmers feed their own people—or nations educate their children and care for the sick—is not mere charity. It's also why the world must come together to confront climate change. There is little scientific dispute that if we do nothing, we will face more drought, more famine, more mass displacement—all of which will fuel more conflict for decades. For this reason, it is not merely scientists and environmental activists who call for swift and forceful action—it's military leaders in my own country and others who understand our common security hangs in the balance.

Agreements among nations. Strong institutions. Support for human rights. Investments in development. All these are vital ingredients in bringing about the evolution that President Kennedy spoke about. And yet, I do not believe that we will have the will, the determination, the staying power, to complete this work without something more—and that's the continued expansion of our moral imagination; an insistence that there's something irreducible that we all share.

As the world grows smaller, you might think it would be easier for human beings to recognize how similar we are; to understand that we're all basically seeking the same things; that we all hope for the chance to live out our lives with some measure of happiness and fulfillment for ourselves and our families.

And yet somehow, given the dizzying pace of globalization, the cultural leveling of modernity, it perhaps comes as no surprise that people fear the loss of what they cherish in their particular identities—their race, their tribe, and perhaps most powerfully their religion. In some places, this fear has led to conflict. At times, it even feels like we're moving backwards. We see it in the Middle East, as the conflict between Arabs and Jews seems to harden. We see it in nations that are torn asunder by tribal lines.

And most dangerously, we see it in the way that religion is used to justify the murder of innocents by those who have distorted and defiled the great religion of Islam, and who attacked my country from Afghanistan. These extremists are not the first to kill in the name of God; the cruelties of the Crusades are amply recorded. But they remind us that no Holy War can ever be a just war. For if you truly believe that you are carrying out divine will, then there is no need for restraint—no need to spare the pregnant mother, or the medic, or the Red Cross worker, or even a person of one's own faith. Such a warped view of religion is not just incompatible with the concept of peace, but I believe it's incompatible with the very purpose of faith—for the one rule that lies at the heart of every major religion is that we do unto others as we would have them do unto us.

Adhering to this law of love has always been the core struggle of human nature. For we are fallible. We make mistakes, and fall victim to the temptations of pride, and power, and sometimes evil. Even those of us with the best of intentions will at times fail to right the wrongs before us.

But we do not have to think that human nature is perfect for us to still believe that the human condition can be perfected. We do not have to live in an idealized world to still reach for those ideals that will make it a better place. The non-violence practiced by men like Gandhi and King may not have been practical or possible in every circumstance, but the love that they preached—their fundamental faith in human progress—that must always be the North Star that guides us on our journey.

For if we lose that faith—if we dismiss it as silly or naïve; if we divorce it from the decisions that we make on issues of war and peace—then we lose what's best about humanity. We lose our sense of possibility. We lose our moral compass.

Like generations have before us, we must reject that future. As Dr. King said at this occasion so many years ago, "I refuse to accept despair as the final response to the ambiguities of history. I refuse to accept the idea that the 'isness' of man's present condition makes him morally incapable of reaching up for the eternal 'oughtness' that forever confronts him."

Let us reach for the world that ought to be—that spark of the divine that still stirs within each of our souls.

Somewhere today, in the here and now, in the world as it is, a soldier sees he's outgunned, but stands firm to keep the peace. Somewhere today, in this world, a young protestor awaits the brutality of her government, but has the courage to march on. Somewhere today, a mother facing punishing poverty still takes the time to teach her child, scrapes together what few coins she has to send that child to school—because she believes that a cruel world still has a place for that child's dreams.

Let us live by their example. We can acknowledge that oppression will always be with us, and still strive for justice. We can admit the intractability of depravation, and still strive for dignity. Clear-eyed, we can understand that there will be war, and still strive for peace. We can do that—for that is the story of human progress; that's the hope of all the world; and at this moment of challenge, that must be our work here on Earth. Thank you very much.

TUCSON MEMORIAL SPEECH

McKALE CENTER
TUCSON, ARIZONA
WEDNESDAY, JANUARY 12, 2011

TO THE FAMILIES of those we've lost, to all who called them friends, to the students of this university, the public servants who are gathered here, the people of Tucson and the people of Arizona: I have come here tonight as an American who, like all Americans, kneels to pray with you today and will stand by you tomorrow.

There is nothing I can say that will fill the sudden hole torn in your hearts. But know this: The hopes of a nation are here tonight. We mourn with you for the fallen. We join you in your grief. And we add our faith to yours that Representative Gabrielle Giffords and the other living victims of this tragedy will pull through.

Scripture tells us, "There is a river whose streams make glad the city of God, the holy place where the most high dwells. God is within her, she will not fall; God will help her at break of day."

On Saturday morning, Gabby, her staff, and many of her constituents gathered outside a supermarket to exercise their right to peaceful assembly and free speech.

They were fulfilling a central tenet of the democracy envisioned by our founders: representatives of the people answering questions to their constituents, so as to carry their concerns back to our nation's capital. Gabby called it "Congress on Your Corner," just an updated version of government of and by and for the people.

And that quintessentially American scene, that was the scene that was shattered by a gunman's bullets. And the six people who lost their lives on Saturday, they, too, represented what is best in us, what is best in America.

Judge John Roll served our legal system for nearly forty years. A graduate of this university and a graduate of this law school...

Judge Roll was recommended for the federal bench by John McCain twenty years ago, appointed by President George H. W. Bush, and rose to become Arizona's chief federal judge.

His colleagues described him as the hardest-working judge within the Ninth Circuit. He was on his way back from attending Mass, as he did every day, when he decided to stop by and say hi to his representative.

John is survived by his loving wife, Maureen, his three sons, and his five beautiful grandchildren.

George and Dorothy Morris—"Dot" to her friends—were high school sweethearts who got married and had two daughters. They did everything together, traveling the open road in their R.V., enjoying what their friends called a fifty-year honeymoon.

Saturday morning, they went by the Safeway to hear what their congresswoman had to say. When gunfire rang out, George, a former Marine, instinctively tried to shield his wife.

Both were shot. Dot passed away.

A New Jersey native, Phyllis Schneck retired to Tucson to beat the snow. But in the summer, she would return east, where her world revolved around her three children, her seven grandchildren, and two-year-old great-granddaughter. A gifted quilter, she'd often work under her favorite tree, or sometimes she'd sew aprons with the logos of the Jets and the Giants...to give out at the church where she volunteered. A Republican, she took a liking to Gabby and wanted to get to know her better.

Dorwan and Mavy Stoddard grew up in Tucson together about seventy years ago. They moved apart and started their own respective families, but after both were widowed, they found their way back here, to, as one of Mavy's daughters put it, "be boyfriend and girlfriend again."

When they weren't out on the road in their motor home, you could find them just up the road, helping folks in need at the Mountain Avenue Church of Christ. A retired construction worker, Dorwan spent his spare time fixing up the church along with their dog, Tux. His final act of selflessness was to dive on top of his wife, sacrificing his life for hers.

Everything—everything Gabe Zimmerman did, he did with passion, but…but his true passion was helping people. As Gabby's outreach director, he made the cares of thousands of her constituents his own, seeing to it that seniors got the Medicare benefits that they had earned, that veterans got the medals and the care that they deserved, that government was working for ordinary folks.

He died doing what he loved: talking with people and seeing how he could help. And Gabe is survived by his parents, Ross and Emily, his brother, Ben, and his fiancee, Kelly, who he planned to marry next year.

And then there is nine-year-old Christina-Taylor Green. Christina was an A student. She was a dancer. She was a gymnast. She was a swimmer. She decided that she wanted to be the first woman to play in the Major Leagues, and as the only girl on her Little League team, no one put it past her.

She showed an appreciation for life uncommon for a girl her age. She'd remind her mother, "We are so blessed. We have the best life." And she'd pay those blessings back by participating in a charity that helped children who were less fortunate.

Our hearts are broken by their sudden passing. Our hearts are broken, and yet our hearts also have reason for fullness.

Our hearts are full of hope and thanks for the thirteen Americans who survived the shooting, including the congresswoman many of them went to see on Saturday. I have just come from the University Medical Center, just a mile from here, where our friend Gabby courageously fights to recover even as we speak.

And I want to tell you—her husband, Mark, is here, and he allows me to share this with you. Right after we went to visit, a few minutes after we left her room and some of her colleagues from Congress were in the room, Gabby opened her eyes for the first time.

Gabby opened her eyes for the first time.

Gabby opened her eyes.

Gabby opened her eyes, so I can tell you, she knows we are here, she knows we love her, and she knows that we are rooting for her through what is undoubtedly going to be a difficult journey. We are there for her.

Our hearts are full of thanks for that good news, and our hearts are full of gratitude for those who saved others. We are grateful to Daniel Hernandez…a volunteer in Gabby's office.

And, Daniel, I'm sorry, you may deny it, but we've decided you are a hero, because you ran through the chaos to minister to your boss and tended to her wounds and help keep her alive.

We are grateful to the men who tackled the gunman as he stopped to reload.

They're right over there.

We—we are grateful for petite Patricia Maisch, who wrestled away the killer's ammunition and undoubtedly saved some lives.

And we are grateful for the doctors and nurses and first responders…who worked wonders to heal those who'd been hurt. We are grateful to them.

These men and women remind us that heroism is found not only on the fields of battle. They remind us that heroism does not require special training or physical strength. Heroism is here, in the hearts of so many of our fellow citizens, all around us, just waiting to be summoned, as it was on Saturday morning.

Their actions, their selflessness poses a challenge to each of us. It raises the question of what, beyond prayers and expressions of concern, is required of us going forward. How can we honor the fallen? How can we be true to their memory?

You see, when a tragedy like this strikes, it is part of our nature to demand explanations, to try to impose some order on the chaos and make sense out of that which seems senseless.

Already, we've seen a national conversation commence, not only about the motivations behind these killings, but about everything from the merits of gun safety laws to the adequacy of our mental health system. And much—much of this process...of debating what might be done to prevent such tragedies in the future is an essential ingredient in our exercise of self-government.

But at a time when our discourse has become so sharply polarized, at a time when we are far too eager to lay the blame for all that ails the world at the feet of those who happen to think differently than we do, it's important for us to pause for a moment and make sure that we're talking with each other in a way that—that heals, not in a way that wounds.

Scripture tells us that there is evil in the world and that terrible things happen for reasons that defy human understanding. In the words of Job, "When I looked for light, then came darkness." Bad things happen, and we have to guard against simple explanations in the aftermath.

For the truth is, none of us can know exactly what triggered this vicious attack. None of us can know with any certainty what might have stopped these shots from being fired or what thoughts lurked in the inner recesses of a violent man's mind.

Yes, we had to examine all the facts behind this tragedy. We cannot and will not be passive in the face of such violence. We should be willing to challenge old assumptions in order to lessen the prospects of such violence in the future.

But what we cannot do is use this tragedy as one more occasion to turn on each other.

That we cannot do.

That we cannot do.

As we discuss these issues, let each of us do so with a good dose of humility. Rather than pointing fingers or assigning blame, let's use this occasion to expand our moral imaginations, to listen to each other more carefully, to sharpen our instincts for empathy, and remind ourselves of all the ways that our hopes and dreams are bound together. After all…

After all, that's what most of us do when we lose somebody in our family, especially if the loss is unexpected. We're shaken out of our routines. We're forced to look inward. We reflect on the past.

Did we spend enough time with an aging—an aging parent, we wonder? Did we express our gratitude for all the sacrifices that they made for us? Did we tell a spouse just how desperately we loved them, not just once in a while, but every single day?

So sudden loss causes us to look backward, but it also forces us to look forward, to reflect on the present and the future, on the manner in which we live our lives and nurture our relationships with those who are still with us.

We may ask ourselves if we've shown enough kindness and generosity and compassion to the people in our lives. Perhaps we question whether we're doing right by our children, or our community, whether our priorities are in order. We recognize our own mortality. And we are reminded that, in the fleeting time we have on this Earth, what matters is not wealth, or status, or power, or fame, but rather how well we have loved and what small part we have played in making the lives of other people better.

And that process—that process of reflection, of making sure we align our values with our actions, that, I believe, is what a tragedy like this requires.

For those who were harmed, those who were killed, they are part of our family, an American family, 300 million strong.

We may not have known them personally, but surely we see ourselves in them. In George and Dot, in Dorwan and Mavy, we sense the abiding love we have for our own husbands, our own wives, our own life partners.

Phyllis, she's our mom or our grandma, Gabe, our brother or son.

In Judge Roll, we recognize not only a man who prized his family and doing his job well, but also a man who embodied America's fidelity to the law.

And in Gabby—in Gabby, we see a reflection of our public-spiritedness, that desire to participate in that sometimes frustrating, sometimes contentious, but always necessary and never-ending process to form a more perfect union.

And in Christina, in Christina, we see all of our children, so curious, so trusting, so energetic, so full of magic, so deserving of our love, and so deserving of our good example.

If this tragedy prompts reflection and debate, as it should, let's make sure it's worthy of those we have lost.

Let's make sure it's not on the usual plane of politics and point-scoring and pettiness that drifts away in the next news cycle.

The loss of these wonderful people should make every one of us strive to be better, to be better in our private lives, to be better friends and neighbors and co-workers and parents.

And if, as has been discussed in recent days, their death helps usher in more civility in our public discourse, let us remember it is not because a simple lack of civility caused this tragedy—it did not—but rather because only a more civil and honest public discourse can help us face up to the challenges of our nation in a way that would make them proud.

We should be civil because we want to live up to the example of public servants like John Roll and Gabby Giffords, who knew first and foremost that we are all Americans, and that we can question each other's ideas without questioning each other's love of country, and that our task, working together, is to constantly widen the circle of our concern so that we bequeath the American dream to future generations.

They believe—they believe and I believe that we can be better. Those who died here, those who saved lives here, they help me believe. We may not be able to stop all evil in the world, but I know that how we treat one another, that's entirely up to us.

And I believe that, for all our imperfections, we are full of decency and goodness and that the forces that divide us are not as strong as those that unite us.

That's what I believe, in part because that's what a child like Christina-Taylor Green believed.

Imagine—can you imagine for a moment, here was a young girl who was just becoming aware of our democracy, just beginning to understand the obligations of citizenship, just starting to glimpse the fact that someday she, too, might play a part in shaping her nation's future.

She had been elected to her student council. She saw public service as something exciting and hopeful. She was off to meet her congresswoman, someone she was sure was good and important and might be a role model. She saw all this through the eyes of a child, undimmed by the cynicism or vitriol that we adults all too often just take for granted.

I want us to live up to her expectations.

I want our democracy to be as good as Christina imagined it. I want America to be as good as she imagined it. All of us, we should do everything we can to make sure this country lives up to our children's expectations.

As has already been mentioned, Christina was given to us on September 11th, 2001, one of fifty babies born that day to be pictured in a book called *Faces of Hope*. On either side of her photo in that book were simple wishes for a child's life: "I hope you help those in need," read one. "I hope you know all of the words to the National Anthem and sing it with your hand over your heart. I hope—I hope you jump in rain puddles."

If there are rain puddles in Heaven, Christina is jumping in them today.

And here on this Earth, here on this Earth, we place our hands over our hearts and we commit ourselves as Americans to forging a country that is forever worthy of her gentle, happy spirit.

May God bless and keep those we've lost in restful and eternal peace. May he love and watch over the survivors. And may he bless the United States of America.

Economics Speech in Osawatomie

OSAWATOMIE HIGH SCHOOL
OSAWATOMIE, KANSAS
TUESDAY, DECEMBER 6, 2011

THANK YOU, EVERYBODY. Please, please have a seat. Thank you so much. Thank you. Good afternoon, everybody.

Well, I want to start by thanking a few folks who've joined us today. We've got the mayor of Osawatomie; Phil Dudley is here. We have your superintendent Gary French in the house. And we have the principal of Osawatomie High, Doug Chisam. And I have brought your former governor, who is doing now an outstanding job as Secretary of Health and Human Services—Kathleen Sebelius is in the house. We love Kathleen.

Well, it is great to be back in the state of Tex—(laughter)—state of Kansas. I was giving Bill Self a hard time; he was here a while back. As many of you know, I have roots here. I'm sure you're all familiar with the Obamas of Osawatomie. Actually, I like to say that I got my name from my father, but I got my accent—and my values—from my mother. She was born in Wichita. Her mother grew up in Augusta. Her father was from El Dorado. So my Kansas roots run deep.

My grandparents served during World War II. He was a soldier in Patton's Army; she was a worker on a bomber assembly line. And together, they shared the optimism of a nation that triumphed over the Great Depression and over fascism. They believed in an America where hard work paid off, and responsibility was rewarded, and anyone could make it if they tried—no matter who you were, no matter where you came from, no matter how you started out.

And these values gave rise to the largest middle class and the strongest economy that the world has ever known. It was here in America that the most productive workers, the most innovative companies turned out the best products on Earth. And you know what? Every American shared in that pride and in that success—from those in the executive suites to those in middle management to those on the factory floor. So you could have some confidence that if you gave it your all, you'd take enough home to raise your family and send your kids to school and have your health care covered, put a little away for retirement.

Today, we're still home to the world's most productive workers. We're still home to the world's most innovative companies. But for most Americans, the basic bargain that made this country great has eroded. Long before the recession hit, hard work stopped paying off for too many people. Fewer and fewer of the folks who contributed to the success of our economy actually benefited from that success. Those at the very top grew wealthier from their incomes and their investments—wealthier than ever before. But everybody else struggled with costs that were growing and paychecks that weren't—and too many families found themselves racking up more and more debt just to keep up.

Now, for many years, credit cards and home equity loans papered over this harsh reality. But in 2008, the house of cards collapsed. We all know the story by now: Mortgages sold to people who couldn't afford them, or even sometimes understand them. Banks and investors allowed to keep packaging the risk and selling it off. Huge bets—and huge bonuses—made with other people's money on the line. Regulators who were supposed to warn us about the dangers of all this, but looked the other way or didn't have the authority to look at all.

It was wrong. It combined the breathtaking greed of a few with irresponsibility all across the system. And it plunged our economy and the world into a crisis from which we're still fighting to recover. It claimed the jobs and the homes and the basic security of millions of people—innocent, hardworking Americans who had met their responsibilities but were still left holding the bag.

And ever since, there's been a raging debate over the best way to restore growth and prosperity, restore balance, restore fairness. Throughout the country, it's sparked protests and political movements—from the tea party to the people who've been occupying the streets of New York and other cities. It's left Washington in a near-constant state of gridlock. It's been the topic of heated and sometimes colorful discussion among the men and women running for president.

But, Osawatomie, this is not just another political debate. This is the defining issue of our time. This is a make-or-break moment for the middle class, and for all those who are fighting to get into the middle class. Because what's at stake is whether this will be a country where working people can earn enough to raise a family, build a modest savings, own a home, secure their retirement.

Now, in the midst of this debate, there are some who seem to be suffering from a kind of collective amnesia. After all that's happened, after the worst economic crisis, the worst financial crisis since the Great Depression, they want to return to the same practices that got us into this mess. In fact, they want to go back to the same policies that stacked the deck against middle-class Americans for way too many years. And their philosophy is simple: We are better off when everybody is left to fend for themselves and play by their own rules.

I am here to say they are wrong. I'm here in Kansas to reaffirm my deep conviction that we're greater together than we are on our own. I believe that this country succeeds when everyone gets a fair shot, when everyone does their fair share, when everyone plays by the same rules. (Applause.) These aren't Democratic values or Republican values. These aren't 1 percent values or 99 percent values. They're American values. And we have to reclaim them.

You see, this isn't the first time America has faced this choice. At the turn of the last century, when a nation of farmers was transitioning to become the world's industrial giant, we had to decide: Would we settle for a country where most of the new railroads and factories were being controlled by a few giant monopolies that kept prices high and wages low? Would we allow our citizens and even our children to work ungodly hours in conditions that were unsafe and unsanitary? Would we restrict education to the privileged few? Because there were people who thought massive inequality and exploitation of people was just the price you pay for progress.

Theodore Roosevelt disagreed. He was the Republican son of a wealthy family. He praised what the titans of industry had done to create jobs and grow the economy. He believed then what we know is true today, that the free market is the greatest force for economic progress in human history. It's led to a prosperity and a standard of living unmatched by the rest of the world.

But Roosevelt also knew that the free market has never been a free license to take whatever you can from whomever you can. He understood the free market only works when there are rules of the road that ensure competition is fair and open and honest. And so he busted up monopolies, forcing those companies to compete for consumers with better services and better prices. And today, they still must. He fought to make sure businesses couldn't profit by exploiting children or selling food or medicine that wasn't safe. And today, they still can't.

And in 1910, Teddy Roosevelt came here to Osawatomie and he laid out his vision for what he called a New Nationalism.

"Our country," he said, "...means nothing unless it means the triumph of a real democracy...of an economic system under which each man shall be guaranteed the opportunity to show the best that there is in him."

Now, for this, Roosevelt was called a radical. He was called a socialist—even a communist. But today, we are a richer nation and a stronger democracy because of what he fought for in his last campaign: an eight-hour work day and a minimum wage for women—insurance for the unemployed and for the elderly, and those with disabilities; political reform and a progressive income tax.

Today, over 100 years later, our economy has gone through another transformation. Over the last few decades, huge advances in technology have allowed businesses to do more with less, and it's made it easier for them to set up shop and hire workers anywhere they want in the world. And many of you know firsthand the painful disruptions this has caused for a lot of Americans.

Factories where people thought they would retire suddenly picked up and went overseas, where workers were cheaper. Steel mills that needed 100—or 1,000 employees are now able to do the same work with 100 employees, so layoffs too often became permanent, not just a temporary part of the business cycle. And these changes didn't just affect blue-collar workers. If you were a bank teller or a phone operator or a travel agent, you saw many in your profession replaced by ATMs and the Internet.

Today, even higher-skilled jobs, like accountants and middle management can be outsourced to countries like China or India. And if you're somebody whose job can be done cheaper by a computer or someone in another country, you don't have a lot of leverage with your employer when it comes to asking for better wages or better benefits, especially since fewer Americans today are part of a union.

Now, just as there was in Teddy Roosevelt's time, there is a certain crowd in Washington who, for the last few decades, have said, let's respond to this economic challenge with the same old tune. "The market will take care of everything," they tell us. If we just cut more regulations and cut more taxes—especially for the wealthy—our economy will grow stronger. Sure, they say, there will be winners and losers. But if the winners do really well, then jobs and prosperity will eventually trickle down to everybody else. And, they argue, even if prosperity doesn't trickle down, well, that's the price of liberty.

Now, it's a simple theory. And we have to admit, it's one that speaks to our rugged individualism and our healthy skepticism of too much government. That's in America's DNA. And that theory fits well on a bumper sticker. But here's the problem: It doesn't work. It has never worked. It didn't work when it was tried in the decade before the Great Depression. It's not what led to the incredible postwar booms of the '50s and '60s. And it didn't work when we tried it during the last decade. I mean, understand, it's not as if we haven't tried this theory.

Remember in those years, in 2001 and 2003, Congress passed two of the most expensive tax cuts for the wealthy in history. And what did it get us? The slowest job growth in half a century. Massive deficits that have made it much harder to pay for the investments that built this country and provided the basic security that helped millions of Americans reach and stay in the middle class—things like education and infrastructure, science and technology, Medicare and Social Security.

Remember that in those same years, thanks to some of the same folks who are now running Congress, we had weak regulation, we had little oversight, and what did it get us? Insurance companies that jacked up people's premiums with impunity and denied care to patients who were sick, mortgage lenders that tricked families into buying homes they couldn't afford, a financial sector where irresponsibility and lack of basic oversight nearly destroyed our entire economy.

We simply cannot return to this brand of "you're on your own" economics if we're serious about rebuilding the middle class in this country. We know that it doesn't result in a strong economy. It results in an economy that invests too little in its people and in its future. We know it doesn't result in a prosperity that trickles down. It results in a prosperity that's enjoyed by fewer and fewer of our citizens.

Look at the statistics. In the last few decades, the average income of the top 1 percent has gone up by more than 250 percent to $1.2 million per year. I'm not talking about millionaires, people who have a million dollars. I'm saying people who make a million dollars every single year. For the top one-hundredth of 1 percent, the average income is now $27 million per year. The typical CEO who used to earn about 30 times more than his or her worker now earns 110 times more. And yet, over the last decade the incomes of most Americans have actually fallen by about 6 percent.

Now, this kind of inequality—a level that we haven't seen since the Great Depression—hurts us all. When middle-class families can no longer afford to buy the goods and services that businesses are selling, when people are slipping out of the middle class, it drags down the entire economy from top to bottom. America was built on the idea of broad-based prosperity, of strong consumers all across the country. That's why a CEO like Henry Ford made it his mission to pay his workers enough so that they could buy the cars he made. It's also why a recent study showed that countries with less inequality tend to have stronger and steadier economic growth over the long run.

Inequality also distorts our democracy. It gives an outsized voice to the few who can afford high-priced lobbyists and unlimited campaign contributions, and it runs the risk of selling out our democracy to the highest bidder. It leaves everyone else rightly suspicious that the system in Washington is rigged against them, that our elected representatives aren't looking out for the interests of most Americans.

But there's an even more fundamental issue at stake. This kind of gaping inequality gives lie to the promise that's at the very heart of America: that this is a place where you can make it if you try. We tell people—we tell our kids—that in this country, even if you're born with nothing, work hard and you can get into the middle class. We tell them that your children will have a chance to do even better than you do. That's why immigrants from around the world historically have flocked to our shores.

And yet, over the last few decades, the rungs on the ladder of opportunity have grown farther and farther apart, and the middle class has shrunk. You know, a few years after World War II, a child who was born into poverty had a slightly better than 50-50 chance of becoming middle class as an adult. By 1980, that chance had fallen to around 40 percent. And if the trend of rising inequality over the last few decades continues, it's estimated that a child born today will only have a one-in-three chance of making it to the middle class—33 percent.

It's heartbreaking enough that there are millions of working families in this country who are now forced to take their children to food banks for a decent meal. But the idea that those children might not have a chance to climb out of that situation and back into the middle class, no matter how hard they work? That's inexcusable. It is wrong. It flies in the face of everything that we stand for.

Now, fortunately, that's not a future that we have to accept, because there's another view about how we build a strong middle class in this country—a view that's truer to our history, a vision that's been embraced in the past by people of both parties for more than 200 years.

It's not a view that we should somehow turn back technology or put up walls around America. It's not a view that says we should punish profit or success or pretend that government knows how to fix all of society's problems. It is a view that says in America we are greater together—when everyone engages in fair play and everybody gets a fair shot and everybody does their fair share.

So what does that mean for restoring middle-class security in today's economy? Well, it starts by making sure that everyone in America gets a fair shot at success. The truth is we'll never be able to compete with other countries when it comes to who's best at letting their businesses pay the lowest wages, who's best at busting unions, who's best at letting companies pollute as much as they want. That's a race to the bottom that we can't win, and we shouldn't want to win that race. Those countries don't have a strong middle class. They don't have our standard of living.

The race we want to win, the race we can win is a race to the top—the race for good jobs that pay well and offer middle-class security. Businesses will create those jobs in countries with the highest-skilled, highest-educated workers, the most advanced transportation and communication, the strongest commitment to research and technology.

The world is shifting to an innovation economy and nobody does innovation better than America. Nobody does it better. No one has better colleges. Nobody has better universities. Nobody has a greater diversity of talent and ingenuity. No one's workers or entrepreneurs are more driven or more daring. The things that have always been our strengths match up perfectly with the demands of the moment.

But we need to meet the moment. We've got to up our game. We need to remember that we can only do that together. It starts by making education a national mission—a national mission. Government and businesses, parents and citizens. In this economy, a higher education is the surest route to the middle class. The unemployment rate for Americans with a college degree or more is about half the national average. And their incomes are twice as high as those who don't have a high school diploma. Which means we shouldn't be laying off good teachers right now—we should be hiring them. We shouldn't be expecting less of our schools—we should be demanding more. We shouldn't be making it harder to afford college—we should be a country where everyone has a chance to go and doesn't rack up $100,000 of debt just because they went.

In today's innovation economy, we also need a world-class commitment to science and research, the next generation of high-tech manufacturing. Our factories and our workers shouldn't be idle. We should be giving people the chance to get new skills and training at community colleges so they can learn how to make wind turbines and semiconductors and high-powered batteries. And by the way, if we don't have an economy that's built on bubbles and financial speculation, our best and brightest won't all gravitate towards careers in banking and finance. Because if we want an economy that's built to last, we need more of those young people in science and engineering. This country should not be known for bad debt and phony profits. We should be known for creating and selling products all around the world that are stamped with three proud words: Made in America.

Today, manufacturers and other companies are setting up shop in the places with the best infrastructure to ship their products, move their workers, communicate with the rest of the world. And that's why the over 1 million construction workers who lost their jobs when the housing market collapsed, they shouldn't be sitting at home with nothing to do. They should be rebuilding our roads and our bridges, laying down faster railroads and broadband, modernizing our schools—all the things other countries are already doing to attract good jobs and businesses to their shores.

Yes, business, and not government, will always be the primary generator of good jobs with incomes that lift people into the middle class and keep them there. But as a nation, we've always come together, through our government, to help create the conditions where both workers and businesses can succeed. And historically, that hasn't been a partisan idea. Franklin Roosevelt worked with Democrats and Republicans to give veterans of World War II—including my grandfather, Stanley Dunham—the chance to go to college on the GI Bill. It was a Republican President, Dwight Eisenhower, a proud son of Kansas—who started the Interstate Highway System, and doubled down on science and research to stay ahead of the Soviets.

Of course, those productive investments cost money. They're not free. And so we've also paid for these investments by asking everybody to do their fair share. Look, if we had unlimited resources, no one would ever have to pay any taxes and we would never have to cut any spending. But we don't have unlimited resources. And so we have to set priorities. If we want a strong middle class, then our tax code must reflect our values. We have to make choices.

Today that choice is very clear. To reduce our deficit, I've already signed nearly $1 trillion of spending cuts into law and I've proposed trillions more, including reforms that would lower the cost of Medicare and Medicaid.

But in order to structurally close the deficit, get our fiscal house in order, we have to decide what our priorities are. Now, most immediately, short term, we need to extend a payroll tax cut that's set to expire at the end of this month. If we don't do that, 160 million Americans, including most of the people here, will see their taxes go up by an average of $1,000 starting in

January and it would badly weaken our recovery. That's the short term.

In the long term, we have to rethink our tax system more fundamentally. We have to ask ourselves: Do we want to make the investments we need in things like education and research and high-tech manufacturing—all those things that helped make us an economic superpower? Or do we want to keep in place the tax breaks for the wealthiest Americans in our country? Because we can't afford to do both. That is not politics. That's just math.

Now, so far, most of my Republican friends in Washington have refused under any circumstance to ask the wealthiest Americans to go to the same tax rate they were paying when Bill Clinton was president. So let's just do a trip down memory lane here.

Keep in mind, when President Clinton first proposed these tax increases, folks in Congress predicted they would kill jobs and lead to another recession. Instead, our economy created nearly 23 million jobs and we eliminated the deficit. Today, the wealthiest Americans are paying the lowest taxes in over half a century. This isn't like in the early '50s, when the top tax rate was over 90 percent. This isn't even like the early '80s, when the top tax rate was about 70 percent. Under President Clinton, the top rate was only about 39 percent. Today, thanks to loopholes and shelters, a quarter of all millionaires now pay lower tax rates than millions of you, millions of middle-class families. Some billionaires have a tax rate as low as 1 percent. One percent.

That is the height of unfairness. It is wrong. It's wrong that in the United States of America, a teacher or a nurse or a construction worker, maybe earns $50,000 a year, should pay a higher tax rate than somebody raking in $50 million. It's wrong for Warren Buffett's secretary to pay a higher tax rate than Warren Buffett. And by the way, Warren Buffett agrees with me. So do most Americans—Democrats, Independents and Republicans. And I know that many of our wealthiest citizens would agree to contribute a little more if it meant reducing the deficit and strengthening the economy that made their success possible.

This isn't about class warfare. This is about the nation's welfare. It's about making choices that benefit not just the people who've done fantastically well over the last few decades, but that benefits the middle class, and those fighting to get into the middle class, and the economy as a whole.

Finally, a strong middle class can only exist in an economy where everyone plays by the same rules, from Wall Street to Main Street. As infuriating as it was for all of us, we rescued our major banks from collapse, not only because a full-blown financial meltdown would have sent us into a second Depression, but because we need a strong, healthy financial sector in this country.

But part of the deal was that we wouldn't go back to business as usual. And that's why last year we put in place new rules of the road that refocus the financial sector on what should be their core purpose: getting capital to the entrepreneurs with the best ideas, and financing millions of families who want to buy a home or send their kids to college.

Now, we're not all the way there yet, and the banks are fighting us every inch of the way. But already, some of these reforms are being implemented.

If you're a big bank or risky financial institution, you now have to write out a "living will" that details exactly how you'll pay the bills if you fail, so that taxpayers are never again on the hook for Wall Street's mistakes. There are also limits on the size of banks and new abilities for regulators to dismantle a firm that is going under. The new law bans banks from making risky bets with their customers' deposits, and it takes away big bonuses and paydays from failed CEOs, while giving shareholders a say on executive salaries.

This is the law that we passed. We are in the process of implementing it now. All of this is being put in place as we speak. Now, unless you're a financial institution whose business model is built on breaking the law, cheating consumers and making risky bets that could damage the entire economy, you should have nothing to fear from these new rules.

Some of you may know, my grandmother worked as a banker for most of her life—worked her way up, started as a secretary, ended up being a vice president of a bank. And I know from her, and I know from all the people that I've come in contact with, that the vast majority of bankers and financial service professionals, they want to do right by their customers. They want to have rules in place that don't put them at a disadvantage for doing the right thing. And yet, Republicans in Congress are fighting as hard as they can to make sure that these rules aren't enforced.

I'll give you a specific example. For the first time in history, the reforms that we passed put in place a consumer watchdog who is charged with protecting everyday Americans from being taken advantage of by mortgage lenders or payday lenders or debt collectors. And the man we nominated for the post, Richard Cordray, is a former attorney general of Ohio who has the support of most attorney generals, both Democrat and Republican, throughout the country. Nobody claims he's not qualified.

But the Republicans in the Senate refuse to confirm him for the job; they refuse to let him do his job. Why? Does anybody here think that the problem that led to our financial crisis was too much oversight of mortgage lenders or debt collectors?

Of course not. Every day we go without a consumer watchdog is another day when a student, or a senior citizen, or a member of our Armed Forces—because they are very vulnerable to some of this stuff—could be tricked into a loan that they can't afford—something that happens all the time. And the fact is that financial institutions have plenty of lobbyists looking out for their interests. Consumers deserve to have someone whose job it is to look out for them. And I intend to make sure they do. And I want you to hear me, Kansas: I will veto any effort to delay or defund or dismantle the new rules that we put in place.

We shouldn't be weakening oversight and accountability. We should be strengthening oversight and accountability. I'll give you another example. Too often, we've seen Wall Street firms violating major anti-fraud laws because the penalties are too weak and there's no price for being a repeat offender. No more. I'll be calling for legislation that makes those penalties count so that firms don't see punishment for breaking the law as just the price of doing business.

The fact is this crisis has left a huge deficit of trust between Main Street and Wall Street. And major banks that were rescued by the taxpayers have an obligation to go the extra mile in helping to close that deficit of trust. At minimum, they should be remedying past mortgage abuses that led to the financial crisis. They should be working to keep responsible homeowners in their home. We're going to keep pushing them to provide more time for unemployed homeowners to look for work without having to worry about immediately losing their house.

The big banks should increase access to refinancing opportunities to borrowers who haven't yet benefited from historically low interest rates. And the big banks should recognize that precisely because these steps are in the interest of middle-class families and the broader economy, it will also be in the banks' own long-term financial interest. What will be good for consumers over the long term will be good for the banks.

Investing in things like education that give everybody a chance to succeed. A tax code that makes sure everybody pays their fair share. And laws that make sure everybody follows the rules. That's what will transform our economy. That's what will grow our middle class again. In the end, rebuilding this economy based on fair play, a fair shot, and a fair share will require all of us to see that we have a stake in each other's success. And it will require all of us to take some responsibility.

It will require parents to get more involved in their children's education. It will require students to study harder. It will require some workers to start studying all over again. It will require greater responsibility from homeowners not to take out mortgages they can't afford. They need to remember that if something seems too good to be true, it probably is.

It will require those of us in public service to make government more efficient and more effective, more consumer-friendly, more responsive to people's needs. That's why we're cutting programs that we don't need to pay for those we do. That's why we've made hundreds of regulatory reforms that will save businesses billions of dollars. That's why we're not just throwing money at education, we're challenging schools to come up with the most innovative reforms and the best results.

And it will require American business leaders to understand that their obligations don't just end with their shareholders. Andy Grove, the legendary former CEO of Intel, put it best. He said, "There is another obligation I feel personally, given that everything I've achieved in my career, and a lot of what Intel has achieved...were made possible by a climate of democracy, an economic climate and investment climate provided by the United States."

This broader obligation can take many forms. At a time when the cost of hiring workers in China is rising rapidly, it should mean more CEOs deciding that it's time to bring jobs back to the United States—not just because it's good for business, but because it's good for the country that made their business and their personal success possible.

I think about the Big Three auto companies who, during recent negotiations, agreed to create more jobs and cars here in America, and then decided to give bonuses not just to their executives, but to all their employees, so that everyone was invested in the company's success.

I think about a company based in Warroad, Minnesota. It's called Marvin Windows and Doors. During the recession, Marvin's competitors closed dozens of plants, let hundreds of workers go. But Marvin's did not lay off a single one of their 4,000 or so employees—not one. In fact, they've only laid off workers once in over a hundred years. Mr. Marvin's grandfather even kept his eight employees during the Great Depression.

Now, at Marvin's when times get tough, the workers agree to give up some perks and some pay, and so do the owners. As one owner said, "You can't grow if you're cutting your lifeblood—and that's the skills and experience your workforce delivers." For the CEO of Marvin's, it's about the community. He said, "These are people we went to school with. We go to church with them. We see them in the same restaurants. Indeed, a lot of us have married local girls and boys. We could be anywhere, but we are in Warroad."

That's how America was built. That's why we're the greatest nation on Earth. That's what our greatest companies understand. Our success has never just been about survival of the fittest. It's about building a nation where we're all better off. We pull together. We pitch in. We do our part. We believe that hard work will pay off, that responsibility will be rewarded, and that our children will inherit a nation where those values live on.

And it is that belief that rallied thousands of Americans to Osawatomie—maybe even some of your ancestors—on a rain-soaked day more than a century ago. By train, by wagon, on buggy, bicycle, on foot, they came to hear the vision of a man who loved this country and was determined to perfect it.

"We are all Americans," Teddy Roosevelt told them that day. "Our common interests are as broad as the continent." In the final years of his life, Roosevelt took that same message all across this country, from tiny Osawatomie to the heart of New York City, believing that no matter where he went, no matter who he was talking to, everybody would benefit from a country in which everyone gets a fair chance.

And well into our third century as a nation, we have grown and we've changed in many ways since Roosevelt's time. The world is faster and the playing field is larger and the challenges are more complex. But what hasn't changed—what can never change—are the values that got us this far. We still have a stake in each other's success. We still believe that this should be a place where you can make it if you try. And we still believe, in the words of the man who called for a New Nationalism all those years ago, "The fundamental rule of our national life," he said, "the rule which underlies all others—is that, on the whole, and in the long run, we shall go up or down together." And I believe America is on the way up.

Thank you. God bless you. God bless the United States of America.

Remarks on the Sandy Hook Elementary Shootings

NEWTOWN HIGH SCHOOL
NEWTOWN, CONNECTICUT
SUNDAY, DECEMBER 16, 2012

THANK YOU. Thank you, Governor. To all the families, first responders, to the community of Newtown, clergy, guests—Scripture tells us: "Do not lose heart. Though outwardly we are wasting away…inwardly we are being renewed day by day. For our light and momentary troubles are achieving for us an eternal glory that far outweighs them all. So we fix our eyes not on what is seen, but on what is unseen, since what is seen is temporary, but what is unseen is eternal. For we know that if the earthly tent we live in is destroyed, we have a building from God, an eternal house in heaven, not built by human hands."

We gather here in memory of twenty beautiful children and six remarkable adults. They lost their lives in a school that could have been any school; in a quiet town full of good and decent people that could be any town in America.

Here in Newtown, I come to offer the love and prayers of a nation. I am very mindful that mere words cannot match the depths of your sorrow, nor can they heal your wounded hearts. I can only hope it helps for you to know that you're not alone in your grief; that our world too has been torn apart; that all across this land of ours, we have wept with you, we've pulled our children tight. And you must know that whatever measure of comfort we can provide, we will provide; whatever portion of sadness that we can share with you to ease this heavy load, we will gladly bear it. Newtown—you are not alone.

As these difficult days have unfolded, you've also inspired us with stories of strength and resolve and sacrifice. We know that when danger arrived in the halls of Sandy Hook Elementary, the school's staff did not flinch, they did not hesitate. Dawn Hochsprung and Mary Sherlach, Vicki Soto, Lauren Rousseau, Rachel D'Avino and Anne Marie Murphy—they responded as we all hope we might respond in such terrifying circumstances—with courage and with love, giving their lives to protect the children in their care.

We know that there were other teachers who barricaded themselves inside classrooms, and kept steady through it all, and reassured their students by saying "wait for the good guys, they're coming"; "show me your smile."

And we know that good guys came. The first responders who raced to the scene, helping to guide those in harm's way to safety, and comfort those in need, holding at bay their own shock and trauma because they had a job to do, and others needed them more.

And then there were the scenes of the schoolchildren, helping one another, holding each other, dutifully following instructions in the way that young children sometimes do; one child even trying to encourage a grown-up by saying, "I know karate. So it's okay. I'll lead the way out."

As a community, you've inspired us, Newtown. In the face of indescribable violence, in the face of unconscionable evil, you've looked out for each other, and you've cared for one another, and you've loved one another. This is how Newtown will be remembered. And with time, and God's grace, that love will see you through.

But we, as a nation, we are left with some hard questions. Someone once described the joy and anxiety of parenthood as the equivalent of having your heart outside of your body all the time, walking around. With their very first cry, this most precious, vital part of ourselves—our child—is suddenly exposed to the world, to possible mishap or malice. And every parent knows there is nothing we will not do to shield our children from harm. And yet, we also know that with that child's very first step, and each step after that, they are separating from us; that we won't—that we can't always be there for them. They'll suffer sickness and setbacks and broken hearts and disappointments. And we learn that our most important job is to give them what they need to become self-reliant and capable and resilient, ready to face the world without fear.

And we know we can't do this by ourselves. It comes as a shock at a certain point where you realize, no matter how much you love these kids, you can't do it by yourself. That this job of keeping our children safe, and teaching them well, is something we can only do together, with the help of friends and neighbors, the help of a community, and the help of a nation. And in that way, we come to realize that we bear a responsibility for every child because we're counting on everybody else to help look after ours; that we're all parents; that they're all our children.

This is our first task—caring for our children. It's our first job. If we don't get that right, we don't get anything right. That's how, as a society, we will be judged.

And by that measure, can we truly say, as a nation, that we are meeting our obligations? Can we honestly say that we're doing enough to keep our children—all of them—safe from harm? Can we claim, as a nation, that we're all together there, letting them know that they are loved, and teaching them to love in return? Can we say that we're truly doing enough to give all the children of this country the chance they deserve to live out their lives in happiness and with purpose?

I've been reflecting on this the last few days, and if we're honest with ourselves, the answer is no. We're not doing enough. And we will have to change.

Since I've been President, this is the fourth time we have come together to comfort a grieving community torn apart by a mass shooting. The fourth time we've hugged survivors. The fourth time we've consoled the families of victims. And in between, there have been an endless series of deadly shootings across the country, almost daily reports of victims, many of them children, in small towns and big cities all across America—victims whose—much of the time, their only fault was being in the wrong place at the wrong time.

We can't tolerate this anymore. These tragedies must end. And to end them, we must change. We will be told that the causes of such violence are complex, and that is true. No single law—no set of laws can eliminate evil from the world, or prevent every senseless act of violence in our society.

But that can't be an excuse for inaction. Surely, we can do better than this. If there is even one step we can take to save another child, or another parent, or another town, from the grief that has visited Tucson, and Aurora, and Oak Creek, and Newtown, and communities from Columbine to Blacksburg before that—then surely we have an obligation to try.

In the coming weeks, I will use whatever power this office holds to engage my fellow citizens—from law enforcement to mental health professionals to parents and educators—in an effort aimed at preventing more tragedies like this. Because what choice do we have? We can't accept events like this as routine. Are we really prepared to say that we're powerless in the face of such carnage, that the politics are too hard? Are we prepared to say that such violence visited on our children year after year after year is somehow the price of our freedom?

All the world's religions—so many of them represented here today—start with a simple question: Why are we here? What gives our life meaning? What gives our acts purpose? We know our time on this Earth is fleeting. We know that we will each have our share of pleasure and pain; that even after we chase after some earthly goal, whether it's wealth or power or fame, or just simple comfort, we will, in some fashion, fall short of what we had hoped. We know that no matter how good our intentions, we will all stumble sometimes, in some way. We will make mistakes, we will experience hardships. And even when we're trying to do the right thing, we know that much of our time will be spent groping through the darkness, so often unable to discern God's heavenly plans.

There's only one thing we can be sure of, and that is the love that we have—for our children, for our families, for each other. The warmth of a small child's embrace—that is true. The memories we have of them, the joy that they bring, the wonder we see through their eyes, that fierce and boundless love we feel for them, a love that takes us out of ourselves, and binds us to something larger—we know that's what matters. We know we're always doing right when we're taking care of them, when we're teaching them well, when we're showing acts of kindness. We don't go wrong when we do that.

That's what we can be sure of. And that's what you, the people of Newtown, have reminded us. That's how you've inspired us. You remind us what matters. And that's what should drive us forward in everything we do, for as long as God sees fit to keep us on this Earth.

"Let the little children come to me," Jesus said, "and do not hinder them—for to such belongs the kingdom of heaven."

Charlotte. Daniel. Olivia. Josephine. Ana. Dylan. Madeleine. Catherine. Chase. Jesse. James. Grace. Emilie. Jack. Noah. Caroline. Jessica. Benjamin. Avielle. Allison.

God has called them all home. For those of us who remain, let us find the strength to carry on, and make our country worthy of their memory.

May God bless and keep those we've lost in His heavenly place. May He grace those we still have with His holy comfort. And may He bless and watch over this community, and the United States of America.

Second Inaugural Address

WASHINGTON, D.C.
MONDAY, JANUARY 21, 2013

VICE PRESIDENT BIDEN, Mr. Chief Justice, Members of the United States Congress, distinguished guests, and fellow citizens:

Each time we gather to inaugurate a president, we bear witness to the enduring strength of our Constitution. We affirm the promise of our democracy. We recall that what binds this nation together is not the colors of our skin or the tenets of our faith or the origins of our names. What makes us exceptional—what makes us American—is our allegiance to an idea, articulated in a declaration made more than two centuries ago:

"We hold these truths to be self-evident, that all men are created equal, that they are endowed by their Creator with certain unalienable rights, that among these are Life, Liberty, and the pursuit of Happiness."

Today we continue a never-ending journey, to bridge the meaning of those words with the realities of our time. For history tells us that while these truths may be self-evident, they have never been self-executing; that while freedom is a gift from God, it must be secured by His people here on Earth. The patriots of 1776 did not fight to replace the tyranny of a king with the privileges of a few or the rule of a mob. They gave to us a Republic, a government of, and by, and for the people, entrusting each generation to keep safe our founding creed.

For more than two hundred years, we have.

Through blood drawn by lash and blood drawn by sword,

we learned that no union founded on the principles of liberty and equality could survive half-slave and half-free. We made ourselves anew, and vowed to move forward together.

Together, we determined that a modern economy requires railroads and highways to speed travel and commerce; schools and colleges to train our workers.

Together, we discovered that a free market only thrives when there are rules to ensure competition and fair play.

Together, we resolved that a great nation must care for the vulnerable, and protect its people from life's worst hazards and misfortune.

Through it all, we have never relinquished our skepticism of central authority, nor have we succumbed to the fiction that all society's ills can be cured through government alone. Our celebration of initiative and enterprise; our insistence on hard work and personal responsibility, these are constants in our character.

But we have always understood that when times change, so must we; that fidelity to our founding principles requires new responses to new challenges; that preserving our individual freedoms ultimately requires collective action. For the American people can no more meet the demands of today's world by acting alone than American soldiers could have met the forces of fascism or communism with muskets and militias. No single person can train all the math and science teachers we'll need to equip our children for the future, or build the roads and networks and research labs that will bring new jobs and businesses to our shores. Now, more than ever, we must do these things together, as one nation, and one people.

This generation of Americans has been tested by crises that steeled our resolve and proved our resilience. A decade of war is now ending. An economic recovery has begun. America's possibilities are limitless, for we possess all the qualities that this world without boundaries demands: youth and drive; diversity and openness; an endless capacity for risk and a gift for reinvention. My fellow Americans, we are made for this moment, and we will seize it—so long as we seize it together.

For we, the people, understand that our country cannot succeed when a shrinking few do very well and a growing many barely make it. We believe that America's prosperity must rest upon the broad shoulders of a rising middle class. We know that America thrives when every person can find independence and pride in their work; when the wages of honest labor liberate families from the brink of hardship. We are true to our creed when a little girl born into the bleakest poverty knows that she has the same chance to succeed as anybody else, because she is an American, she is free, and she is equal, not just in the eyes of God but also in our own.

We understand that outworn programs are inadequate to the needs of our time. So we must harness new ideas and technology to remake our government, revamp our tax code, reform our schools, and empower our citizens with the skills they need to work harder, learn more, reach higher. But while the means will change, our purpose endures: a nation that rewards the effort and determination of every single American. That is what this moment requires. That is what will give real meaning to our creed.

We, the people, still believe that every citizen deserves a basic measure of security and dignity. We must make the hard choices to reduce the cost of health care and the size of our deficit. But we reject the belief that America must choose between caring for the generation that built this country and investing in the generation that will build its future. For we remember the lessons of our past, when twilight years were spent in poverty, and parents of a child with a disability had nowhere to turn. We do not believe that in this country, freedom is reserved for the lucky, or happiness for the few. We recognize that no matter how responsibly we live our lives, any one of us, at any time, may face a job loss, or a sudden illness, or a home swept away in a terrible storm. The commitments we make to each other—through Medicare, and Medicaid, and Social Security—these things do not sap our initiative; they strengthen us. They do not make us a nation of takers; they free us to take the risks that make this country great.

We, the people, still believe that our obligations as Americans are not just to ourselves, but to all posterity. We will respond to the threat of climate change, knowing that the failure to do so would betray our children and future generations. Some may still deny the overwhelming judgment of science, but none can avoid the devastating impact of raging fires, and crippling drought, and more powerful storms. The path towards sustainable energy sources will be long and sometimes difficult. But America cannot resist this transition; we must lead it. We cannot cede to other nations the technology that will power new jobs and new industries—we must claim its promise. That is how we will maintain our economic vitality and our national treasure—our forests and waterways; our croplands and snowcapped peaks. That is how we will preserve our planet, commanded to our care by God. That's what will lend meaning to the creed our fathers once declared.

We, the people, still believe that enduring security and lasting peace do not require perpetual war. Our brave men and women in uniform, tempered by the flames of battle, are unmatched in skill and courage. Our citizens, seared by the memory of those we have lost, know too well the price that is paid for liberty. The knowledge of their sacrifice will keep us forever vigilant against those who would do us harm. But we are also heirs to those who won the peace and not just the war, who turned sworn enemies into the surest of friends, and we must carry those lessons into this time as well.

We will defend our people and uphold our values through strength of arms and rule of law. We will show the courage to try and resolve our differences with other nations peacefully—not because we are naïve about the dangers we face, but because engagement can more durably lift suspicion and fear. America will remain the anchor of strong alliances in every corner of the globe; and we will renew those institutions that extend our capacity to manage crisis abroad, for no one has a greater stake in a peaceful world than its most powerful nation. We will support democracy from Asia to Africa; from the Americas to the Middle East, because our interests and our conscience compel us to act on behalf of those who long for freedom. And we must be a source of hope to the poor, the sick, the marginalized, the victims of prejudice—not out of mere charity, but because peace in our time requires the constant advance of those principles that our common creed describes: tolerance and opportunity; human dignity and justice.

We, the people, declare today that the most evident of truths—that all of us are created equal—is the star that guides us still; just as it guided our forebears through Seneca Falls, and Selma, and Stonewall; just as it guided all those men and women, sung and unsung, who left footprints along this great Mall, to hear a preacher say that we cannot walk alone; to hear a King proclaim that our individual freedom is inextricably bound to the freedom of every soul on Earth.

It is now our generation's task to carry on what those pioneers began. For our journey is not complete until our wives, our mothers, and daughters can earn a living equal to their efforts. Our journey is not complete until our gay brothers and sisters are treated like anyone else under the law—for if we are truly created equal, then surely the love we commit to one another must be equal as well. Our journey is not complete until no citizen is forced to wait for hours to exercise the right to vote. Our journey is not complete until we find a better way to welcome the striving, hopeful immigrants who still see America as a land of opportunity; until bright young students and engineers are enlisted in our workforce rather than expelled from our country. Our journey is not complete until all our children, from the streets of Detroit to the hills of Appalachia to the quiet lanes of Newtown, know that they are cared for, and cherished, and always safe from harm.

That is our generation's task—to make these words, these rights, these values—of Life, and Liberty, and the Pursuit of Happiness—real for every American. Being true to our founding documents does not require us to agree on every contour of life; it does not mean we will all define liberty in exactly the same way, or follow the same precise path to happiness. Progress does not compel us to settle centuries-long debates about the role of government for all time—but it does require us to act in our time.

For now decisions are upon us, and we cannot afford delay. We cannot mistake absolutism for principle, or substitute spectacle for politics, or treat name-calling as reasoned debate. We must act; we must act knowing that our work will be imperfect. We must act, knowing that today's victories will be only partial, and that it will be up to those who stand here in four years, and forty years, and four hundred years hence to advance the timeless spirit once conferred to us in a spare Philadelphia hall.

My fellow Americans, the oath I have sworn before you today, like the one recited by others who serve in this Capitol, was an oath to God and country, not party or faction—and we must faithfully execute that pledge during the duration of our service. But the words I spoke today are not so different from the oath that is taken each time a soldier signs up for duty, or an immigrant realizes her dream. My oath is not so different from the pledge we all make to the flag that waves above and that fills our hearts with pride.

They are the words of citizens, and they represent our greatest hope.

You and I, as citizens, have the power to set this country's course.

You and I, as citizens, have the obligation to shape the debates of our time—not only with the votes we cast, but with the voices we lift in defense of our most ancient values and enduring ideals.

Let each of us now embrace, with solemn duty and awesome joy, what is our lasting birthright. With common effort and common purpose, with passion and dedication, let us answer the call of history, and carry into an uncertain future that precious light of freedom.

Thank you, God bless you, and may He forever bless these United States of America.

Remarks at the 50th Anniversary of the Selma Marches

EDMUND PETTUS BRIDGE
SELMA, ALABAMA
SUNDAY, MARCH 7, 2015

IT IS A RARE HONOR in this life to follow one of your heroes. And John Lewis is one of my heroes.

Now, I have to imagine that when a younger John Lewis woke up that morning fifty years ago and made his way to Brown Chapel, heroics were not on his mind. A day like this was not on his mind. Young folks with bedrolls and backpacks were milling about. Veterans of the movement trained newcomers in the tactics of non-violence; the right way to protect yourself when attacked. A doctor described what tear gas does to the body, while marchers scribbled down instructions for contacting their loved ones. The air was thick with doubt, anticipation and fear. And they comforted themselves with the final verse of the final hymn they sung:

> "No matter what may be the test, God will take care of you;
> Lean, weary one, upon His breast, God will take care of you."

And then, his knapsack stocked with an apple, a toothbrush, and a book on government—all you need for a night behind bars—John Lewis led them out of the church on a mission to change America.

President and Mrs. Bush, Governor Bentley, Mayor Evans, Sewell, Reverend Strong, members of Congress, elected officials, foot soldiers, friends, fellow Americans:

As John noted, there are places and moments in America where this nation's destiny has been decided. Many are sites of war—Concord and Lexington, Appomattox, Gettysburg. Others are sites that symbolize the daring of America's character—Independence Hall and Seneca Falls, Kitty Hawk and Cape Canaveral.

Selma is such a place. In one afternoon fity years ago, so much of our turbulent history—the stain of slavery and anguish of civil war; the yoke of segregation and tyranny of Jim Crow; the death of four little girls in Birmingham; and the dream of a Baptist preacher—all that history met on this bridge.

It was not a clash of armies, but a clash of wills; a contest to determine the true meaning of America. And because of men and women like John Lewis, Joseph Lowery, Hosea Williams, Amelia Boynton, Diane Nash, Ralph Abernathy, C. T. Vivian, Andrew Young, Fred Shuttlesworth, Dr. Martin Luther King Jr., and so many others, the idea of a just America and a fair America, an inclusive America, and a generous America—that idea ultimately triumphed.

As is true across the landscape of American history, we cannot examine this moment in isolation. The march on Selma was part of a broader campaign that spanned generations; the leaders that day part of a long line of heroes.

We gather here to celebrate them. We gather here to honor the courage of ordinary Americans willing to endure billy clubs and the chastening rod; tear gas and the trampling hoof; men and women who despite the gush of blood and splintered bone would stay true to their North Star and keep marching towards justice.

They did as Scripture instructed: "Rejoice in hope, be patient in tribulation, be constant in prayer." And in the days to come, they went back again and again. When the trumpet call sounded for more to join, the people came—black and white, young and old, Christian and Jew, waving the American flag and singing the same anthems full of faith and hope. A white newsman, Bill Plante, who covered the marches then and who is with us here today, quipped that the growing number of white people lowered the quality of the singing. To those who marched, though, those old gospel songs must have never sounded so sweet.

In time, their chorus would well up and reach President Johnson. And he would send them protection, and speak to the nation, echoing their call for America and the world to hear: "We shall overcome." What enormous faith these men and women had. Faith in God, but also faith in America.

The Americans who crossed this bridge, they were not physically imposing. But they gave courage to millions. They held no elected office. But they led a nation. They marched as Americans who had endured hundreds of years of brutal violence, countless daily indignities—but they didn't seek special treatment, just the equal treatment promised to them almost a century before.

What they did here will reverberate through the ages. Not because the change they won was preordained; not because their victory was complete; but because they proved that nonviolent change is possible, that love and hope can conquer hate.

As we commemorate their achievement, we are well-served to remember that at the time of the marches, many in power condemned rather than praised them. Back then, they were called Communists, or half-breeds, or outside agitators, sexual and moral degenerates, and worse—they were called everything but the name their parents gave them. Their faith was questioned. Their lives were threatened. Their patriotism challenged.

And yet, what could be more American than what happened in this place? What could more profoundly vindicate the idea of America than plain and humble people—unsung, the downtrodden, the dreamers not of high station, not born to wealth or privilege, not of one religious tradition but many, coming together to shape their country's course?

What greater expression of faith in the American experiment than this, what greater form of patriotism is there than the belief that America is not yet finished, that we are strong enough to be self-critical, that each successive generation can look upon our imperfections and decide that it is in our power to remake this nation to more closely align with our highest ideals?

That's why Selma is not some outlier in the American experience. That's why it's not a museum or a static monument to behold from a distance. It is instead the manifestation of a creed written into our founding documents: "We the People... in order to form a more perfect union." "We hold these truths to be self-evident, that all men are created equal."

These are not just words. They're a living thing, a call to action, a roadmap for citizenship and an insistence in the capacity of free men and women to shape our own destiny. For founders like Franklin and Jefferson, for leaders like Lincoln and FDR, the success of our experiment in self-government rested on engaging all of our citizens in this work. And that's what we celebrate here in Selma. That's what this movement was all about, one leg in our long journey toward freedom.

The American instinct that led these young men and women to pick up the torch and cross this bridge, that's the same instinct that moved patriots to choose revolution over tyranny. It's the same instinct that drew immigrants from across oceans and the Rio Grande; the same instinct that led women to reach for the ballot, workers to organize against an unjust status quo; the same instinct that led us to plant a flag at Iwo Jima and on the surface of the Moon.

It's the idea held by generations of citizens who believed that America is a constant work in progress; who believed that loving this country requires more than singing its praises or avoiding uncomfortable truths. It requires the occasional disruption, the willingness to speak out for what is right, to shake up the status quo. That's America.

That's what makes us unique. That's what cements our reputation as a beacon of opportunity. Young people behind the Iron Curtain would see Selma and eventually tear down that wall. Young people in Soweto would hear Bobby Kennedy talk about ripples of hope and eventually banish the scourge of apartheid. Young people in Burma went to prison rather than submit to military rule. They saw what John Lewis had done. From the streets of Tunis to the Maidan in Ukraine, this generation of young people can draw strength from this place, where the powerless could change the world's greatest power and push their leaders to expand the boundaries of freedom.

They saw that idea made real right here in Selma, Alabama. They saw that idea manifest itself here in America.

Because of campaigns like this, a Voting Rights Act was passed. Political and economic and social barriers came down. And the change these men and women wrought is visible here today in the presence of African Americans who run boardrooms, who sit on the bench, who serve in elected office from small towns to big cities; from the Congressional Black Caucus all the way to the Oval Office.

Because of what they did, the doors of opportunity swung open not just for black folks, but for every American. Women marched through those doors. Latinos marched through those doors. Asian Americans, gay Americans, Americans with disabilities—they all came through those doors. Their endeavors gave the entire South the chance to rise again, not by reasserting the past, but by transcending the past.

What a glorious thing, Dr. King might say. And what a solemn debt we owe. Which leads us to ask, just how might we repay that debt?

First and foremost, we have to recognize that one day's commemoration, no matter how special, is not enough. If Selma taught us anything, it's that our work is never done. The American experiment in self-government gives work and purpose to each generation.

Selma teaches us, as well, that action requires that we shed our cynicism. For when it comes to the pursuit of justice, we can afford neither complacency nor despair.

Just this week, I was asked whether I thought the Department of Justice's Ferguson report shows that, with respect to race, little has changed in this country. And I understood the question; the report's narrative was sadly familiar. It evoked the kind of abuse and disregard for citizens that spawned the Civil Rights Movement. But I rejected the notion that nothing's changed. What happened in Ferguson may not be unique, but it's no longer endemic. It's no longer sanctioned by law or by custom. And before the Civil Rights Movement, it most surely was.

We do a disservice to the cause of justice by intimating that bias and discrimination are immutable, that racial division is inherent to America. If you think nothing's changed in the past fifty years, ask somebody who lived through the Selma or Chicago or Los Angeles of the 1950s. Ask the female CEO who once might have been assigned to the secretarial pool if nothing's changed. Ask your gay friend if it's easier to be out and proud in America now than it was thirty years ago.

To deny this progress, this hard-won progress—our progress—would be to rob us of our own agency, our own capacity, our responsibility to do what we can to make America better.

Of course, a more common mistake is to suggest that Ferguson is an isolated incident; that racism is banished; that the work that drew men and women to Selma is now complete, and that whatever racial tensions remain are a consequence of those seeking to play the "race card" for their own purposes. We don't need the Ferguson report to know that's not true. We just need to open our eyes, and our ears, and our hearts to know that this nation's racial history still casts its long shadow upon us.

We know the march is not yet over. We know the race is not yet won. We know that reaching that blessed destination where we are judged, all of us, by the content of our character requires admitting as much, facing up to the truth. "We are capable of bearing a great burden," James Baldwin once wrote, "once we discover that the burden is reality and arrive where reality is."

There's nothing America can't handle if we actually look squarely at the problem. And this is work for all Americans, not just some. Not just whites. Not just blacks. If we want to honor the courage of those who marched that day, then all of us are called to possess their moral imagination. All of us will need to feel as they did the fierce urgency of now. All of us need to recognize as they did that change depends on our actions, on our attitudes, the things we teach our children. And if we make such an effort, no matter how hard it may sometimes seem, laws can be passed, and consciences can be stirred, and consensus can be built.

With such an effort, we can make sure our criminal justice system serves all and not just some. Together, we can raise the level of mutual trust that policing is built on—the idea that police officers are members of the community they risk their lives to protect, and citizens in Ferguson and New York and Cleveland, they just want the same thing young people here marched for fifty years ago—the protection of the law. Together, we can address unfair sentencing and overcrowded prisons, and the stunted circumstances that rob too many boys of the chance to become men, and rob the nation of too many men who could be good dads, and good workers, and good neighbors.

With effort, we can roll back poverty and the roadblocks to opportunity. Americans don't accept a free ride for anybody, nor do we believe in equality of outcomes. But we do expect equal opportunity. And if we really mean it, if we're not just giving lip service to it, but if we really mean it and are willing to sacrifice for it, then, yes, we can make sure every child gets an education suitable to this new century, one that expands imaginations and lifts sights and gives those children the skills they need. We can make sure every person willing to work has the dignity of a job, and a fair wage, and a real voice, and sturdier rungs on that ladder into the middle class.

And with effort, we can protect the foundation stone of our democracy for which so many marched across this bridge—and that is the right to vote. Right now, in 2015, fifty years after Selma, there are laws across this country designed to make it harder for people to vote. As we speak, more of such laws are being proposed. Meanwhile, the Voting Rights Act, the culmination of so much blood, so much sweat and tears, the product of so much sacrifice in the face of wanton violence, the Voting Rights Act stands weakened, its future subject to political rancor.

How can that be? The Voting Rights Act was one of the crowning achievements of our democracy, the result of Republican and Democratic efforts. President Reagan signed its renewal when he was in office. President George W. Bush signed its renewal when he was in office. One hundred members of Congress have come here today to honor people who were willing to die for the right to protect it. If we want to honor this day, let that hundred go back to Washington and gather four hundred more, and together, pledge to make it their mission to restore that law this year. That's how we honor those on this bridge.

Of course, our democracy is not the task of Congress alone, or the courts alone, or even the President alone. If every new voter-suppression law was struck down today, we would still have, here in America, one of the lowest voting rates among free peoples. Fifty years ago, registering to vote here in Selma and much of the South meant guessing the number of jellybeans in a jar, the number of bubbles on a bar of soap. It meant risking your dignity, and sometimes, your life.

What's our excuse today for not voting? How do we so casually discard the right for which so many fought? How do we so fully give away our power, our voice, in shaping America's future? Why are we pointing to somebody else when we could take the time just to go to the polling places? We give away our power.

Fellow marchers, so much has changed in fifty years. We have endured war and we've fashioned peace. We've seen technological wonders that touch every aspect of our lives. We take for granted conveniences that our parents could have scarcely imagined. But what has not changed is the imperative of citizenship; that willingness of a twenty-six-year-old deacon, or a Unitarian minister, or a young mother of five to decide they loved this country so much that they'd risk everything to realize its promise.

That's what it means to love America. That's what it means to believe in America. That's what it means when we say America is exceptional.

For we were born of change. We broke the old aristocracies, declaring ourselves entitled not by bloodline, but endowed by our Creator with certain inalienable rights. We secure our rights and responsibilities through a system of self-government, of and by and for the people. That's why we argue and fight with so much passion and conviction—because we know our efforts matter. We know America is what we make of it.

Look at our history. We are Lewis and Clark and Sacajawea, pioneers who braved the unfamiliar, followed by a stampede of farmers and miners, and entrepreneurs and hucksters. That's our spirit. That's who we are.

We are Sojourner Truth and Fannie Lou Hamer, women who could do as much as any man and then some. And we're Susan B. Anthony, who shook the system until the law reflected that truth. That is our character.

We're the immigrants who stowed away on ships to reach these shores, the huddled masses yearning to breathe free— Holocaust survivors, Soviet defectors, the Lost Boys of Sudan. We're the hopeful strivers who cross the Rio Grande because we want our kids to know a better life. That's how we came to be.

We're the slaves who built the White House and the economy of the South. We're the ranch hands and cowboys who opened up the West, and countless laborers who laid rail, and raised skyscrapers, and organized for workers' rights.

We're the fresh-faced GIs who fought to liberate a continent. And we're the Tuskegee Airmen, and the Navajo code-talkers, and the Japanese Americans who fought for this country even as their own liberty had been denied.

We're the firefighters who rushed into those buildings on 9/11, the volunteers who signed up to fight in Afghanistan and Iraq. We're the gay Americans whose blood ran in the streets of San Francisco and New York, just as blood ran down this bridge.

We are storytellers, writers, poets, artists who abhor unfairness, and despise hypocrisy, and give voice to the voiceless, and tell truths that need to be told.

We're the inventors of gospel and jazz and blues, bluegrass and country, and hip-hop and rock and roll, and our very own sound with all the sweet sorrow and reckless joy of freedom.

We are Jackie Robinson, enduring scorn and spiked cleats and pitches coming straight to his head, and stealing home in the World Series anyway.

We are the people Langston Hughes wrote of who "build our temples for tomorrow, strong as we know how." We are the people Emerson wrote of, "who for truth and honor's sake stand fast and suffer long;" who are "never tired, so long as we can see far enough."

That's what America is. Not stock photos or airbrushed history, or feeble attempts to define some of us as more American than others. We respect the past, but we don't pine for the past. We don't fear the future; we grab for it. America is not some fragile thing. We are large, in the words of Whitman, containing multitudes. We are boisterous and diverse and full of energy, perpetually young in spirit. That's why someone like John Lewis at the ripe old age of twenty-five could lead a mighty march.

And that's what the young people here today and listening all across the country must take away from this day. You are America. Unconstrained by habit and convention. Unencumbered by what is, because you're ready to seize what ought to be.

For everywhere in this country, there are first steps to be taken, there's new ground to cover, there are more bridges to be crossed. And it is you, the young and fearless at heart, the most diverse and educated generation in our history, who the nation is waiting to follow.

Because Selma shows us that America is not the project of any one person. Because the single most powerful word in our democracy is the word "We." "We the People." "We Shall Overcome." "Yes We Can." That word is owned by no one. It belongs to everyone. Oh, what a glorious task we are given, to continually try to improve this great nation of ours.

Fifty years from Bloody Sunday, our march is not yet finished, but we're getting closer. Two hundred and thirty-nine years after this nation's founding our union is not yet perfect, but we are getting closer. Our job's easier because somebody already got us through that first mile. Somebody already got us over that bridge. When it feels the road is too hard, when the torch we've been passed feels too heavy, we will remember these early travelers, and draw strength from their example, and hold firmly the words of the prophet Isaiah: "Those who hope in the Lord will renew their strength. They will soar on [the] wings like eagles. They will run and not grow weary. They will walk and not be faint."

We honor those who walked so we could run. We must run so our children soar. And we will not grow weary. For we believe in the power of an awesome God, and we believe in this country's sacred promise.

May He bless those warriors of justice no longer with us, and bless the United States of America. Thank you, everybody.

Charleston Shooting Eulogy

WHITE HOUSE BRIEFING ROOM
WASHINGTON, D.C.
SUNDAY, JUNE 18, 2015

Good afternoon, everybody.

THIS MORNING, I spoke with and Vice President Biden spoke with Mayor Joe Riley and other leaders at Charleston to express our deep sorrow over the senseless murders that took place last night.

Michelle and I know several members of Emanuel AME Church. We knew their pastor, Reverend Clementa Pinckney, who, along with eight others, gathered in prayer and fellowship and was murdered last night, and to say our thoughts and prayers are with them and their families and their community doesn't say enough to convey the heartache and the sadness and the anger that we feel.

Any death of this sort is a tragedy. Any shooting involving multiple victims is a tragedy. There is something particularly heartbreaking about a death happening in a place in which we seek solace and we seek peace, in a place of worship.

Mother Emanuel is, in fact, more than a church. This is a place of worship that was founded by African Americans seeking liberty. This is a church that was burned to the ground because its worshipers worked to end slavery.

When there were laws banning all-black church gatherings, they conducted church services in secret. When there was a nonviolent movement to bring our country in closer line with our highest ideals, some of our brightest leaders spoke and led marches from this church's steps.

This is a sacred place in the history of Charleston and in the history of America.

The FBI is now on the scene with local police, and more of the bureau's best are on their way to join them. The attorney general has announced plans for the FBI to open a hate crime investigation. We understand that the suspect is in custody, and I'll let the best of law enforcement do its work to make sure that justice is served.

Until the investigation is complete, I'm necessarily constrained in terms of talking about the details of the case. But I don't need to be constrained about the emotions that tragedies like this raise.

I've had to make statements like this too many times. Communities like this have had to endure tragedies like this too many times.

We don't have all the facts, but we do know that once again, innocent people were killed in part because someone who wanted to inflict harm had no trouble getting their hand on a gun.

Now is the time for mourning and for healing. But let's be clear. At some point, we as a country will have to reckon with the fact that this type of mass violence does not happen in other advanced countries. It doesn't happen in other places with this kind of frequency.

And it is in our power to do something about it. I say that recognizing the politics in this town foreclose a lot of those avenues right now. But it'd be wrong for us not to acknowledge it, and at some point, it's going to be important for the American people to come to grips with it and for us to be able to shift how we think about the issue of gun violence collectively.

The fact that this took place in a black church obviously also raises questions about a dark part of our history. This is not the first time that black churches have been attacked, and we know the hatred across races and faiths pose a particular threat to our democracy and our ideals.

The good news is I am confident that the outpouring of unity and strength and fellowship and love across Charleston today, from all races, from all faiths, from all places of worship, indicates the degree to which those old vestiges of hatred can be overcome.

That certainly was Dr. King's hope just over fifty years ago after four little girls were killed in a bombing at a black church in Birmingham, Alabama.

He said, "They lived meaningful lives, and they died nobly. They say to each of us," Dr. King said, "black and white alike, that we must substitute courage for caution. They say to us that we must be concerned not merely with who murdered them but about the system, the way of life, philosophy which produced the murders. Their death says to us that we must work passionately and unrelentingly for the realization of the American Dream.

"And if one will hold on, he will discover that God walks with him and that God is able to lift you from the fatigue of despair to the buoyancy of hope and transform dark and desolate valleys into sunlit paths of inner peace."

Reverend Pinckney and his congregation understood that spirit. Their Christian faith compelled them to reach out not just to members of their congregation or to members of their own communities but to all in need. They opened their doors to strangers who might enter a church in search of healing or redemption.

Mother Emanuel Church and its congregation have risen before from flames, from an earthquake, from other dark times to give hope to generations of Charlestonians, and with our prayers and our love and the buoyancy of hope, it will rise again now as a place of peace.

Thank you.

Commencement Address

RUTGERS UNIVERSITY
BRUNSWICK, NEW JERSEY
SATURDAY, MAY 15, 2016

HELLO RUTGERS! R-U rah-rah! Thank you so much. Thank you. Everybody, please have a seat. Thank you, President Barchi, for that introduction. Let me congratulate my extraordinarily worthy fellow honorary Scarlet Knights, Dr. Burnell and Bill Moyers.

Matthew, good job. If you are interested, we can talk after this.

One of the perks of my job is honorary degrees. But I have to tell you, it impresses nobody in my house. Now Malia and Sasha just say, "Okay, Dr. Dad, we'll see you later. Can we have some money?"

To the Board of Governors; to Chairman Brown; to Lieutenant Governor Guadagno; Mayor Cahill; Mayor Wahler, members of Congress, Rutgers administrators, faculty, staff, friends, and family—thank you for the honor of joining you for the 250th anniversary of this remarkable institution. But most of all, congratulations to the Class of 2016!

I come here for a simple reason—to finally settle this pork roll vs. Taylor ham question. I'm just kidding. There's not much I'm afraid to take on in my final year of office, but I know better than to get in the middle of that debate.

The truth is, Rutgers, I came here because you asked. Now, it's true that a lot of schools invite me to their commencement every year. But you are the first to launch a three-year campaign. E-mails, letters, tweets, YouTube videos. I even got three notes from the grandmother of your student body president. And I have to say that really sealed the deal. That was smart, because I have a soft spot for grandmas.

So I'm here, off Exit 9, on the banks of the Old Raritan —at the site of one of the original nine colonial colleges. Winners of the first-ever college football game. One of the newest members of the Big Ten. Home of what I understand to be a Grease Truck for a Fat Sandwich. Mozzarella sticks and chicken fingers on your cheesesteaks—I'm sure Michelle would approve.

But somehow, you have survived such death-defying acts. You also survived the daily jockeying for buses, from Livingston to Busch, to Cook, to Douglass, and back again. I suspect that a few of you are trying to survive this afternoon, after a late night at Olde Queens. You know who you are.

But, however you got here, you made it. You made it. Today, you join a long line of Scarlet Knights whose energy and intellect have lifted this university to heights its founders could not have imagined. Two hundred and fifty years ago, when America was still just an idea, a charter from the Royal Governor—Ben Franklin's son—established Queen's College. A few years later, a handful of students gathered in a converted tavern for the first class. And from that first class in a pub, Rutgers has evolved into one of the finest research institutions in America.

This is a place where you 3D-print prosthetic hands for children, and devise rooftop wind arrays that can power entire office buildings with clean, renewable energy. Every day, tens of thousands of students come here, to this intellectual melting pot, where ideas and cultures flow together among what might just be America's most diverse student body. Here in New Brunswick, you can debate philosophy with a classmate from South Asia in one class, and then strike up a conversation on the EE Bus with a first-generation Latina student from Jersey

City, before sitting down for your psych group project with a veteran who's going to school on the Post-9/11 GI Bill.

America converges here. And in so many ways, the history of Rutgers mirrors the evolution of America—the course by which we became bigger, stronger, and richer and more dynamic, and a more inclusive nation.

But America's progress has never been smooth or steady. Progress doesn't travel in a straight line. It zigs and zags in fits and starts. Progress in America has been hard and contentious, and sometimes bloody. It remains uneven and at times, for every two steps forward, it feels like we take one step back.

Now, for some of you, this may sound like your college career. It sounds like mine, anyway. Which makes sense, because measured against the whole of human history, America remains a very young nation—younger, even, than this university.

But progress is bumpy. It always has been. But because of dreamers and innovators and strivers and activists, progress has been this nation's hallmark. I'm fond of quoting Dr. Martin Luther King Jr., who said, "The arc of the moral universe is long, but it bends towards justice." It bends towards justice. I believe that. But I also believe that the arc of our nation, the arc of the world does not bend towards justice, or freedom, or equality, or prosperity on its own. It depends on us, on the choices we make, particularly at certain inflection points in history; particularly when big changes are happening and everything seems up for grabs.

And, Class of 2016, you are graduating at such an inflection point. Since the start of this new millennium, you've already witnessed horrific terrorist attacks, and war, and a Great Recession.

You've seen economic and technological and cultural shifts that are profoundly altering how we work and how we communicate, how we live, how we form families. The pace of change is not subsiding; it is accelerating. And these changes offer not only great opportunity, but also great peril.

Fortunately, your generation has everything it takes to lead this country toward a brighter future. I'm confident that you can make the right choices—away from fear and division and paralysis, and toward cooperation and innovation and hope. Now, partly, I'm confident because, on average, you're smarter and better educated than my generation—although we probably had better penmanship—and were certainly better spellers. We did not have spell-check back in my day. You're not only better educated, you've been more exposed to the world, more exposed to other cultures. You're more diverse. You're more environmentally conscious. You have a healthy skepticism for conventional wisdom.

So you've got the tools to lead us. And precisely because I have so much confidence in you, I'm not going to spend the remainder of my time telling you exactly how you're going to make the world better. You'll figure it out. You'll look at things with fresher eyes, unencumbered by the biases and blind spots and inertia and general crankiness of your parents and grandparents and old heads like me. But I do have a couple of suggestions that you may find useful as you go out there and conquer the world.

Point number one: When you hear someone longing for the "good old days," take it with a grain of salt. Take it with a grain of salt. We live in a great nation and we are rightly proud of our history. We are beneficiaries of the labor and the grit and the courage of generations who came before. But I guess it's part of human nature, especially in times of change and uncertainty, to want to look backwards and long for some imaginary past when everything worked, and the economy hummed, and all politicians were wise, and every kid was well-mannered, and

America pretty much did whatever it wanted around the world. Guess what. It ain't so. The "good old days" weren't that great. Yes, there have been some stretches in our history where the economy grew much faster, or when government ran more smoothly. There were moments when, immediately after World War II, for example, or the end of the Cold War, when the world bent more easily to our will. But those are sporadic, those moments, those episodes. In fact, by almost every measure, America is better, and the world is better, than it was 50 years ago, or 30 years ago, or even 8 years ago.

And by the way, I'm not—set aside 150 years ago, pre–Civil War—there's a whole bunch of stuff there we could talk about. Set aside life in the '50s, when women and people of color were systematically excluded from big chunks of American life. Since I graduated, in 1983—which isn't that long ago— I'm just saying. Since I graduated, crime rates, teenage pregnancy, the share of Americans living in poverty—they're all down. The share of Americans with college educations have gone way up. Our life expectancy has, as well. Blacks and Latinos have risen up the ranks in business and politics. More women are in the workforce. They're earning more money—although it's long past time that we passed laws to make sure that women are getting the same pay for the same work as men.

Meanwhile, in the eight years since most of you started high school, we're also better off. You and your fellow graduates are entering the job market with better prospects than any time since 2007. Twenty million more Americans know the financial security of health insurance. We're less dependent on foreign oil. We've doubled the production of clean energy. We have cut the high school dropout rate. We've cut the deficit by two-thirds. Marriage equality is the law of the land.

And just as America is better, the world is better than when I graduated. Since I graduated, an Iron Curtain fell, apartheid ended. There's more democracy. We virtually eliminated certain diseases like polio. We've cut extreme poverty drastically. We've cut infant mortality by an enormous amount.

Now, I say all these things not to make you complacent. We've got a bunch of big problems to solve. But I say it to point out that change has been a constant in our history. And the reason America is better is because we didn't look backwards, we didn't fear the future. We seized the future and made it our own. And that's exactly why it's always been young people like you that have brought about big change—because you don't fear the future.

That leads me to my second point: The world is more interconnected than ever before, and it's becoming more connected every day. Building walls won't change that.

Look, as President, my first responsibility is always the security and prosperity of the United States. And as citizens, we all rightly put our country first. But if the past two decades have taught us anything, it's that the biggest challenges we face cannot be solved in isolation. When overseas states start falling apart, they become breeding grounds for terrorists and ideologies of nihilism and despair that ultimately can reach our shores. When developing countries don't have functioning health systems, epidemics like Zika or Ebola can spread and threaten Americans, too. And a wall won't stop that.

If we want to close loopholes that allow large corporations and wealthy individuals to avoid paying their fair share of taxes, we've got to have the cooperation of other countries in a global financial system to help enforce financial laws. The point is, to help ourselves we've got to help others —not pull up the drawbridge and try to keep the world out.

And engagement does not just mean deploying our military. There are times where we must take military action to protect ourselves and our allies, and we are in awe of and we are grateful for the men and women who make up the finest fighting force the world has ever known. But I worry if we think that the entire burden of our engagement with the world is up to the 1 percent who serve in our military, and the rest of us can just sit back and do nothing. They can't shoulder the entire burden. And engagement means using all the levers of our national power, and rallying the world to take on our shared challenges.

You look at something like trade, for example. We live in an age of global supply chains, and cargo ships that crisscross oceans, and online commerce that can render borders obsolete. And a lot of folks have legitimate concerns with the way globalization has progressed— that's one of the changes that's been taking place—jobs shipped overseas, trade deals that sometimes put workers and businesses at a disadvantage. But the answer isn't to stop trading with other countries. In this global economy, that's not even possible. The answer is to do trade the right way, by negotiating with other countries so that they raise their labor standards and their environmental standards; and we make sure they don't impose unfair tariffs on American goods or steal American intellectual property. That's how we make sure that international rules are consistent with our values—including human rights. And ultimately, that's how we help raise wages here in America. That's how we help our workers compete on a level playing field.

Building walls won't do that. It won't boost our economy, and it won't enhance our security either. Isolating or disparaging Muslims, suggesting that they should be treated differently when it comes to entering this country—that is not just a betrayal of our values—that's not just a betrayal of who we are, it would alienate the very communities at home and abroad who are our most important partners in the fight against violent extremism. Suggesting that we can build an endless wall along our borders, and blame our challenges on immigrants—that doesn't just run counter to our history as the world's melting pot; it contradicts the evidence that our growth and our innovation and our dynamism has always been spurred by our ability to attract strivers from every corner of the globe. That's how we became America. Why would we want to stop it now?

Which brings me to my third point: Facts, evidence, reason, logic, an understanding of science—these are good things. These are qualities you want in people making policy. These are qualities you want to continue to cultivate in yourselves as citizens. That might seem obvious. That's why we honor Bill Moyers or Dr. Burnell.

We traditionally have valued those things. But if you were listening to today's political debate, you might wonder where this strain of anti-intellectualism came from. So, Class of 2016, let me be as clear as I can be. In politics and in life, ignorance is not a virtue. It's not cool to not know what you're talking about. That's not keeping it real, or telling it like it is. That's not challenging political correctness. That's just not knowing what you're talking about. And yet, we've become confused about this.

Look, our nation's Founders—Franklin, Madison, Hamilton, Jefferson—they were born of the Enlightenment. They sought to escape superstition, and sectarianism, and tribalism, and know-nothingness. They believed in rational thought and experimentation, and the capacity of informed citizens to master our own fates. That is embedded in our constitutional design. That spirit informed our inventors and our explorers, the Edisons and the Wright Brothers, and the George Washington Carvers and the Grace Hoppers, and the Norman Borlaugs and the Steve Jobses. That's what built this country.

And today, in every phone in one of your pockets—we have access to more information than at any time in human history, at a touch of a button. But, ironically, the flood of information hasn't made us more discerning of the truth. In some ways, it's just made us more confident in our ignorance. We assume whatever is on the web must be true. We search for sites that just reinforce our own predispositions. Opinions masquerade as facts. The wildest conspiracy theories are taken for gospel.

Now, understand, I am sure you've learned during your years of college—and if not, you will learn soon—that there are a whole lot of folks who are book smart and have no common sense. That's the truth. You'll meet them if you haven't already. So the fact that they've got a fancy degree—you got to talk to them to see whether they know what they're talking about. Qualities like kindness and compassion, honesty, hard work—they often matter more than technical skills or know-how.

But when our leaders express a disdain for facts, when they're not held accountable for repeating falsehoods and just making stuff up, while actual experts are dismissed as elitists, then we've got a problem.

You know, it's interesting that if we get sick, we actually want to make sure the doctors have gone to medical school, they know what they're talking about. If we get on a plane, we say we really want a pilot to be able to pilot the plane. And yet, in our public lives, we certainly think, "I don't want somebody who's done it before." The rejection of facts, the rejection of reason and science—that is the path to decline. It calls to mind the words of Carl Sagan, who graduated high school here in New Jersey—he said: "We can judge our progress by the courage of our questions and the depths of our answers, our willingness to embrace what is true rather than what feels good."

The debate around climate change is a perfect example of this. Now, I recognize it doesn't feel like the planet is warmer right now. I understand. There was hail when I landed in Newark. (The wind starts blowing hard.) But think about the climate change issue. Every day, there are officials in high office with responsibilities who mock the overwhelming consensus of the world's scientists that human activities and the release of carbon dioxide and methane and other substances are altering our climate in profound and dangerous ways.

A while back, you may have seen a United States senator trotted out a snowball during a floor speech in the middle of winter as "proof" that the world was not warming. I mean, listen, climate change is not something subject to political spin. There is evidence. There are facts. We can see it happening right now. If we don't act, if we don't follow through on the progress we made in Paris, the progress we've been making here at home, your generation will feel the brunt of this catastrophe.

So it's up to you to insist upon and shape an informed debate. Imagine if Benjamin Franklin had seen that senator with the snowball, what he would think. Imagine if your fifth grade science teacher had seen that. He'd get a D. And he's a senator!

Look, I'm not suggesting that cold analysis and hard data are ultimately more important in life than passion, or faith, or love, or loyalty. I am suggesting that those highest expressions of our humanity can only flourish when our economy functions well, and proposed budgets add up, and our environment is protected. And to accomplish those things, to make collective decisions on behalf of a common good, we have to use our heads. We have to agree that facts and evidence matter. And we got to hold our leaders and ourselves accountable to know what the heck they're talking about.

All right. I only have two more points. I know it's getting cold and you guys have to graduate. Point four: Have faith in democracy. Look, I know it's not always pretty. Really, I know. I've been living it. But it's how, bit by bit, generation by generation, we have made progress in this nation. That's how we banned child labor. That's how we cleaned up our air and our water. That's how we passed programs like Social Security and Medicare that lifted millions of seniors out of poverty.

None of these changes happened overnight. They didn't happen because some charismatic leader got everybody suddenly to agree on everything. It didn't happen because some massive political revolution occurred. It actually happened over the course of years of advocacy, and organizing, and alliance-building, and deal-making, and the changing of public opinion. It happened because ordinary Americans who cared participated in the political process.

Look, if you want to change this country for the better, you better start participating. I'll give you an example on a lot of people's minds right now—and that's the growing inequality in our economy. Over much of the last century, we've unleashed the strongest economic engine the world has ever seen, but over the past few decades, our economy has become more and more unequal. The top 10 percent of earners now take in half of all income in the U.S. In the past, it used to be a top CEO made 20 or 30 times the income of the average worker. Today, it's 300 times more. And wages aren't rising fast enough for millions of hardworking families.

Now, if we want to reverse those trends, there are a bunch of policies that would make a real difference. We can raise the minimum wage. We can modernize our infrastructure. We can invest in early childhood education. We can make college more affordable. We can close tax loopholes on hedge fund managers and take that money and give tax breaks to help families with child care or retirement. And if we did these things, then we'd help to restore the sense that hard work is rewarded and we could build an economy that truly works for everybody.

Now, the reason some of these things have not happened, even though the majority of people approve of them, is really simple. It's not because I wasn't proposing them. It wasn't because the facts and the evidence showed they wouldn't work. It was because a huge chunk of Americans, especially young people, do not vote.

In 2014, voter turnout was the lowest since World War II. Fewer than one in five young people showed up to vote—2014. And the four who stayed home determined the course of this country just as much as the single one who voted. Because apathy has consequences. It determines who our Congress is. It determines what policies they prioritize. It even, for example, determines whether a really highly qualified Supreme Court nominee receives the courtesy of a hearing and a vote in the United States Senate.

And, yes, big money in politics is a huge problem. We've got to reduce its influence. Yes, special interests and lobbyists have disproportionate access to the corridors of power. But, contrary to what we hear sometimes from both the left as well as the right, the system isn't as rigged as you think, and it certainly is not as hopeless as you think. Politicians care about being elected, and they especially care about being reelected. And if you vote and you elect a majority that represents your views, you will get what you want. And if you opt out, or stop paying attention, you won't. It's that simple. It's not that complicated.

Now, one of the reasons that people don't vote is because they don't see the changes they were looking for right away. Well, guess what—none of the great strides in our history happened right away. It took Thurgood Marshall and the NAACP decades to win *Brown v. Board of Education*; and then another decade after that to secure the Civil Rights Act and the Voting Rights Act. And it took more time after that for it to start working. It took a proud daughter of New Jersey, Alice Paul, years of organizing marches and hunger strikes and protests, and drafting hundreds of pieces of legislation, and writing letters and giving speeches, and working with congressional leaders before she and other suffragettes finally helped win women the right to vote.

Each stage along the way required compromise. Sometimes you took half a loaf. You forged allies. Sometimes you lost on an issue, and then you came back to fight another day. That's how democracy works. So you've got to be committed to participating not just if you get immediate gratification, but you got to be a citizen full-time, all the time.

And if participation means voting, and it means compromise, and organizing and advocacy, it also means listening to those who don't agree with you. I know a couple years ago, folks on this campus got upset that Condoleezza Rice was supposed to speak at a commencement. Now, I don't think it's a secret that I disagree with many of the foreign policies of Dr. Rice and the previous administration. But the notion that this community or the country would be better served by not hearing from a former Secretary of State, or shutting out what she had to say—I believe that's misguided. I don't think that's how democracy works best, when we're not even willing to listen to each other. I believe that's misguided.

If you disagree with somebody, bring them in—and ask them tough questions. Hold their feet to the fire. Make them defend their positions. If somebody has got a bad or offensive idea, prove it wrong. Engage it. Debate it. Stand up for what you believe in. Don't be scared to take somebody on. Don't feel like you got to shut your ears off because you're too fragile and somebody might offend your sensibilities. Go at them if they're not making any sense. Use your logic and reason and words. And by doing so, you'll strengthen your own position, and you'll hone your arguments. And maybe you'll learn something and realize you don't know everything. And you may have a new understanding not only about what your opponents believe but maybe what you believe. Either way, you win. And more importantly, our democracy wins.

So, anyway, all right. That's it, Class of 2016—a few suggestions on how you can change the world. Except maybe I've got one last suggestion. Just one. And that is, gear yourself for the long haul. Whatever path you choose—business, nonprofits, government, education, health care, the arts—whatever it is, you're going to have some setbacks. You will deal occasionally with foolish people. You will be frustrated. You'll have a boss that's not great. You won't always get everything you want—at least not as fast as you want it. So you have to stick with it. You have to be persistent. And success, however small, however incomplete, success is still success. I always tell my daughters, you know, better is good. It may not be perfect, it may not be great, but it's good. That's how progress happens—in societies and in our own lives.

So don't lose hope if sometimes you hit a roadblock. Don't lose hope in the face of naysayers. And certainly don't let resistance make you cynical. Cynicism is so easy, and cynics don't accomplish much. As a friend of mine who happens to be from New Jersey, a guy named Bruce Springsteen, once sang— "they spend their lives waiting for a moment that just don't come." Don't let that be you. Don't waste your time waiting.

If you doubt you can make a difference, look at the impact some of your fellow graduates are already making. Look at what Matthew is doing. Look at somebody like Yasmin Ramadan, who began organizing anti-bullying assemblies when she was ten years old to help kids handle bias and discrimination, and here at Rutgers, helped found the Muslim Public Relations Council to work with administrators and police to promote inclusion.

Look at somebody like Madison Little, who grew up dealing with some health issues, and started wondering what his care would have been like if he lived someplace else, and so, here at Rutgers, he took charge of a student nonprofit and worked with folks in Australia and Cambodia and Uganda to address the AIDS epidemic. "Our generation has so much energy to adapt and impact the world," he said. "My peers give me a lot of hope that we'll overcome the obstacles we face in society."

That's you! Is it any wonder that I am optimistic? Throughout our history, a new generation of Americans has reached up and bent the arc of history in the direction of more freedom, and more opportunity, and more justice. And, Class of 2016, it is your turn now—to shape our nation's destiny, as well as your own.

So get to work. Make sure the next 250 years are better than the last.

Good luck. God bless you. God bless this country we love. Thank you.

Democratic National Convention Speech

PHILADELPHIA, PENNSYLVANIA
WEDNESDAY, JULY 27, 2016

Hello, America.

TWELVE YEARS AGO TONIGHT, I addressed this convention for the very first time.

You met my two little girls, Malia and Sasha—now two amazing young women who just fill me with pride. You fell for my brilliant wife and partner Michelle, who's made me a better father and a better man; who's gone on to inspire our nation as First Lady; and who somehow hasn't aged a day.

I know the same can't be said for me. My girls remind me all the time. Wow, you've changed so much, Daddy.

And it's true—I was so young that first time in Boston. Maybe a little nervous addressing such a big crowd. But I was filled with faith; faith in America—the generous, bighearted, hopeful country that made my story—indeed, all of our stories—possible.

A lot's happened over the years. And while this nation has been tested by war and recession and all manner of challenge—I stand before you again tonight, after almost two terms as your President, to tell you I am even more optimistic about the future of America.

How could I not be—after all we've achieved together?

After the worst recession in eighty years, we've fought our way back. We've seen deficits come down, 401(k)s recover, an auto industry set new records, unemployment reach eight-year lows, and our businesses create 15 million new jobs.

After a century of trying, we declared that health care in America is not a privilege for a few, but a right for everybody. After decades of talk, we finally began to wean ourselves off foreign oil, and doubled our production of clean energy.

We brought more of our troops home to their families, and delivered justice to Osama bin Laden. Through diplomacy, we shut down Iran's nuclear weapons program, opened up a new chapter with the people of Cuba, and brought nearly 200 nations together around a climate agreement that could save this planet for our kids.

We put policies in place to help students with loans; protect consumers from fraud; and cut veteran homelessness almost in half. And through countless acts of quiet courage, America learned that love has no limits, and marriage equality is now a reality across the land.

By so many measures, our country is stronger and more prosperous than it was when we started.

And through every victory and every setback, I've insisted that change is never easy, and never quick; that we wouldn't meet all of our challenges in one term, or one presidency, or even in one lifetime.

So tonight, I'm here to tell you that yes, we still have more work to do. More work to do for every American still in need of a good job or a raise, paid leave or a decent retirement; for every child who needs a sturdier ladder out of poverty or a world-class education; for everyone who hasn't yet felt the progress of these past seven and a half years. We need to keep making our streets safer and our criminal justice system fairer; our homeland more secure, and our world more peaceful and sustainable for the next generation. We're not done perfecting our union, or living up to our founding creed—that all of us are created equal and free in the eyes of God.

That work involves a big choice this November. Fair to say, this is not your typical election. It's not just a choice between parties or policies; the usual debates between left and right. This is a more fundamental choice—about who we are as a people, and whether we stay true to this great American experiment in self-government.

Look, we Democrats have always had plenty of differences with the Republican Party, and there's nothing wrong with that; it's precisely this contest of ideas that pushes our country forward.

But what we heard in Cleveland last week wasn't particularly Republican—and it sure wasn't conservative. What we heard was a deeply pessimistic vision of a country where we turn against each other, and turn away from the rest of the world. There were no serious solutions to pressing problems—just the fanning of resentment, and blame, and anger, and hate.

And that is not the America I know.

The America I know is full of courage, and optimism, and ingenuity. The America I know is decent and generous. Sure, we have real anxieties—about paying the bills, protecting our kids, caring for a sick parent. We get frustrated with political gridlock, worry about racial divisions; are shocked and saddened by the madness of Orlando or Nice. There are pockets of America that never recovered from factory closures; men who took pride in hard work and providing for their families who now feel forgotten; parents who wonder whether their kids will have the same opportunities we had.

All that is real. We're challenged to do better; to be better. But as I've traveled this country, through all fifty states; as I've rejoiced with you and mourned with you, what I've also seen, more than anything, is what is right with America. I see people working hard and starting businesses; people teaching kids and serving our country. I see engineers inventing stuff, and doctors coming up with new cures. I see a younger generation full of energy and new ideas, not constrained by what is, ready to seize what ought to be.

Most of all, I see Americans of every party, every background, every faith who believe that we are stronger together—black, white, Latino, Asian, Native American; young and old; gay, straight, men, women, folks with disabilities, all pledging allegiance, under the same proud flag, to this big, bold country that we love.

That's the America I know. And there is only one candidate in this race who believes in that future, and has devoted her life to it; a mother and grandmother who'd do anything to help our children thrive; a leader with real plans to break down barriers, blast through glass ceilings, and widen the circle of opportunity to every single American—the next President of the United States, Hillary Clinton.

Now, eight years ago, Hillary and I were rivals for the Democratic nomination. We battled for a year and a half. Let me tell you, it was tough, because Hillary's tough. Every time I thought I might have that race won, Hillary just came back stronger.

But after it was all over, I asked Hillary to join my team. She was a little surprised, but ultimately said yes—because she knew that what was at stake was bigger than either of us. And for four years, I had a front-row seat to her intelligence, her judgment, and her discipline. I came to realize that her unbelievable work ethic wasn't for praise or attention—that she was in this for everyone who needs a champion. I understood that after all these years, she has never forgotten just who she's fighting for.

Hillary's still got the tenacity she had as a young woman working at the Children's Defense Fund, going door to door to ultimately make sure kids with disabilities could get a quality education.

She's still got the heart she showed as our First Lady, working with Congress to help push through a Children's Health Insurance Program that to this day protects millions of kids.

She's still seared with the memory of every American she met who lost loved ones on 9/11, which is why, as a Senator from New York, she fought so hard for funding to help first responders; why, as Secretary of State, she sat with me in the Situation Room and forcefully argued in favor of the mission that took out bin Laden.

You know, nothing truly prepares you for the demands of the Oval Office. Until you've sat at that desk, you don't know what it's like to manage a global crisis, or send young people to war. But Hillary's been in the room; she's been part of those decisions. She knows what's at stake in the decisions our government makes for the working family, the senior citizen, the small business owner, the soldier, and the veteran. Even in the middle of crisis, she listens to people, and keeps her cool, and treats everybody with respect. And no matter how daunting the odds; no matter how much people try to knock her down, she never, ever quits.

That's the Hillary I know. That's the Hillary I've come to admire. And that's why I can say with confidence there has never been a man or a woman more qualified than Hillary Clinton to serve as President of the United States of America.

And, by the way, in case you were wondering about her judgment, look at her choice of running mate. Tim Kaine is as good a man, as humble and committed a public servant, as anyone I know. He will be a great Vice President, and he'll make Hillary a better President. Just like my dear friend and brother Joe Biden has made me a better President.

Now, Hillary has real plans to address the concerns she's heard from you on the campaign trail. She's got specific ideas to invest in new jobs, to help workers share in their company's profits, to help put kids in preschool, and put students through college without taking on a ton of debt. That's what leaders do.

And then there's Donald Trump. He's not really a plans guy. Not really a facts guy, either. He calls himself a business guy, which is true, but I have to say, I know plenty of businessmen and women who've achieved success without leaving a trail of lawsuits, and unpaid workers, and people feeling like they got cheated.

Does anyone really believe that a guy who's spent his seventy years on this Earth showing no regard for working people is suddenly going to be your champion? Your voice? If so, you should vote for him. But if you're someone who's truly concerned about paying your bills, and seeing the economy grow, and creating more opportunity for everybody, then the choice isn't even close. If you want someone with a lifelong track record of fighting for higher wages, better benefits, a fairer tax code, a bigger voice for workers, and stronger regulations on Wall Street, then you should vote for Hillary Clinton.

And if you're concerned about who's going to keep you and your family safe in a dangerous world—well, the choice is even clearer. Hillary Clinton is respected around the world not just by leaders, but by the people they serve. She's worked closely with our intelligence teams, our diplomats, our military. And she has the judgment, the experience, and the temperament to meet the threat from terrorism. It's not new to her. Our troops have pounded ISIL without mercy, taking out leaders, taking back territory. I know Hillary won't relent until ISIL is destroyed. She'll finish the job—and she'll do it without resorting to torture, or banning entire religions from entering our country. She is fit to be the next Commander-in-Chief.

Meanwhile, Donald Trump calls our military a disaster. Apparently, he doesn't know the men and women who make up the strongest fighting force the world has ever known. He suggests America is weak. He must not hear the billions of men, women, and children, from the Baltics to Burma, who still look to America to be the light of freedom, dignity, and human rights. He cozies up to Putin, praises Saddam Hussein, and tells the NATO allies that stood by our side after 9/11 that they have to pay up if they want our protection. Well, America's promises do not come with a price tag. We meet our commitments. And that's one reason why almost every country on Earth sees America as stronger and more respected today than they did eight years ago.

America is already great. America is already strong. And I promise you, our strength, our greatness, does not depend on Donald Trump.

In fact, it doesn't depend on any one person. And that, in the end, may be the biggest difference in this election—the meaning of our democracy.

Ronald Reagan called America "a shining city on a hill." Donald Trump calls it "a divided crime scene" that only he can fix. It doesn't matter to him that illegal immigration and the crime rate are as low as they've been in decades, because he's not offering any real solutions to those issues. He's just offering slogans, and he's offering fear. He's betting that if he scares enough people, he might score just enough votes to win this election.

That is another bet that Donald Trump will lose. Because he's selling the American people short. We are not a fragile or frightful people. Our power doesn't come from some self-declared savior promising that he alone can restore order. We don't look to be ruled. Our power comes from those immortal declarations first put to paper right here in Philadelphia all those years ago: We hold these truths to be self-evident, that all men are created equal; that together, We, the People, can form a more perfect union.

That's who we are. That's our birthright—the capacity to shape our own destiny. That's what drove patriots to choose revolution over tyranny and our GIs to liberate a continent. It's what gave women the courage to reach for the ballot, and marchers to cross a bridge in Selma, and workers to organize and fight for better wages.

America has never been about what one person says he'll do for us. It's always been about what can be achieved by us, together, through the hard, slow, sometimes frustrating, but ultimately enduring work of self-government.

And that's what Hillary Clinton understands. She knows that this is a big, diverse country, and that most issues are rarely black and white. That even when you're 100 percent right, getting things done requires compromise. That democracy doesn't work if we constantly demonize each other. She knows that for progress to happen, we have to listen to each other, see ourselves in each other, fight for our principles but also fight to find common ground, no matter how elusive that may seem.

Hillary knows we can work through racial divides in this country when we realize the worry black parents feel when their son leaves the house isn't so different than what a brave cop's family feels when he puts on the blue and goes to work; that we can honor police and treat every community fairly. She knows that acknowledging problems that have festered for decades isn't making race relations worse—it's creating the possibility for people of good will to join and make things better.

Hillary knows we can insist on a lawful and orderly immigration system while still seeing striving students and their toiling parents as loving families, not criminals or rapists; families that came here for the same reasons our forebears came—to work, and study, and make a better life, in a place where we can talk and worship and love as we please. She knows their dream is quintessentially American, and the American Dream is something no wall will ever contain.

It can be frustrating, this business of democracy. Trust me, I know. Hillary knows, too. When the other side refuses to compromise, progress can stall. Supporters can grow impatient, and worry that you're not trying hard enough; that you've maybe sold out.

But I promise you, when we keep at it; when we change enough minds; when we deliver enough votes, then progress does happen. Just ask the 20 million more people who have health care today. Just ask the Marine who proudly serves his country without hiding the husband he loves. Democracy works, but we gotta want it—not just during an election year, but all the days in between.

So if you agree that there's too much inequality in our economy, and too much money in our politics, we all need to be as vocal and as organized and as persistent as Bernie Sanders' supporters have been. We all need to get out and vote for Democrats up and down the ticket, and then hold them accountable until they get the job done.

If you want more justice in the justice system, then we've all got to vote—not just for a President, but for mayors, and sheriffs, and state's attorneys, and state legislators. And we've got to work with police and protesters until laws and practices are changed.

If you want to fight climate change, we've got to engage not only young people on college campuses, but reach out to the coal miner who's worried about taking care of his family, the single mom worried about gas prices.

If you want to protect our kids and our cops from gun violence, we've got to get the vast majority of Americans, including gun owners, who agree on background checks to be just as vocal and determined as the gun lobby that blocks change through every funeral we hold. That's how change will happen.

Look, Hillary's got her share of critics. She's been caricatured by the right and by some folks on the left; accused of everything you can imagine—and some things you can't. But she knows that's what happens when you're under a microscope for forty years. She knows she's made mistakes, just like I have; just like we all do. That's what happens when we try. That's what happens when you're the kind of citizen Teddy Roosevelt once described—not the timid souls who criticize from the sidelines, but someone "who is actually in the arena…who strives valiantly; who errs…[but] who at the best knows in the end the triumph of high achievement."

Hillary Clinton is that woman in the arena. She's been there for us—even if we haven't always noticed. And if you're serious about our democracy, you can't afford to stay home just because she might not align with you on every issue. You've got to get in the arena with her, because democracy isn't a spectator sport. America isn't about "yes he will." It's about "yes we can." And we're going to carry Hillary to victory this fall, because that's what the moment demands.

You know, there's been a lot of talk in this campaign about what America's lost—people who tell us that our way of life is being undermined by pernicious changes and dark forces beyond our control. They tell voters there's a "real America" out there that must be restored. This isn't an idea that started with Donald Trump. It's been peddled by politicians for a long time—probably from the start of our Republic.

And it's got me thinking about the story I told you twelve years ago tonight, about my Kansas grandparents and the things they taught me when I was growing up. They came from the heartland; their ancestors began settling there about 200 years ago. They were Scotch-Irish mostly, farmers, teachers, ranch hands, pharmacists, oil rig workers. Hardy, small town folks. Some were Democrats, but a lot of them were Republicans. My grandparents explained that they didn't like show-offs. They didn't admire braggarts or bullies. They didn't respect mean-spiritedness, or folks who were always looking for shortcuts in life. Instead, they valued traits like honesty and hard work. Kindness and courtesy. Humility; responsibility; helping each other out.

That's what they believed in. True things. Things that last. The things we try to teach our kids.

And what my grandparents understood was that these values weren't limited to Kansas. They weren't limited to small towns. These values could travel to Hawaii; even the other side of the world, where my mother would end up working to help poor women get a better life. They knew these values weren't reserved for one race; they could be passed down to a half-Kenyan grandson, or a half-Asian granddaughter; in fact, they were the same values Michelle's parents, the descendants of slaves, taught their own kids living in a bungalow on the South Side of Chicago. They knew these values were exactly what drew immigrants here, and they believed that the children of those immigrants were just as American as their own, whether they wore a cowboy hat or a yarmulke; a baseball cap or a hijab.

America has changed over the years. But these values my grandparents taught me—they haven't gone anywhere. They're as strong as ever; still cherished by people of every party, every race, and every faith. They live on in each of us. What makes us American, what makes us patriots, is what's in here. That's what matters. That's why we can take the food and music and holidays and styles of other countries, and blend it into something uniquely our own. That's why we can attract strivers and entrepreneurs from around the globe to build new factories and create new industries here. That's why our military can look the way it does, every shade of humanity, forged into common service. That's why anyone who threatens our values, whether fascists or communists or jihadists or homegrown demagogues, will always fail in the end.

That's America. Those bonds of affection; that common creed. We don't fear the future; we shape it, embrace it, as one people, stronger together than we are on our own. That's what Hillary Clinton understands—this fighter, this stateswoman, this mother and grandmother, this public servant, this patriot—that's the America she's fighting for.

And that's why I have confidence, as I leave this stage tonight, that the Democratic Party is in good hands. My time in this office hasn't fixed everything; as much as we've done, there's still so much I want to do. But for all the tough lessons I've had to learn; for all the places I've fallen short; I've told Hillary, and I'll tell you what's picked me back up, every single time.

It's been you. The American people.

It's the letter I keep on my wall from a survivor in Ohio who twice almost lost everything to cancer, but urged me to keep fighting for health care reform, even when the battle seemed lost. Do not quit.

It's the painting I keep in my private office, a big-eyed, green owl, made by a seven-year-old girl who was taken from us in Newtown, given to me by her parents so I wouldn't forget—a reminder of all the parents who have turned their grief into action.

It's the small business owner in Colorado who cut most of his own salary so he wouldn't have to lay off any of his workers in the recession—because, he said, "that wouldn't have been in the spirit of America."

It's the conservative in Texas who said he disagreed with me on everything, but appreciated that, like him, I try to be a good dad.

It's the courage of the young soldier from Arizona who nearly died on the battlefield in Afghanistan, but who's learned to speak and walk again—and earlier this year, stepped through the door of the Oval Office on his own power, to salute and shake my hand.

It's every American who believed we could change this country for the better, so many of you who'd never been involved in politics, who picked up phones, and hit the streets, and used the Internet in amazing new ways to make change happen. You are the best organizers on the planet, and I'm so proud of all the change you've made possible.

Time and again, you've picked me up. I hope, sometimes, I picked you up, too. Tonight, I ask you to do for Hillary Clinton what you did for me. I ask you to carry her the same way you carried me. Because you're who I was talking about twelve years ago, when I talked about hope—it's been you who've fueled my dogged faith in our future, even when the odds are great; even when the road is long. Hope in the face of difficulty; hope in the face of uncertainty; the audacity of hope!

America, you have vindicated that hope these past eight years. And now I'm ready to pass the baton and do my part as a private citizen. This year, in this election, I'm asking you to join me—to reject cynicism, reject fear, to summon what's best in us; to elect Hillary Clinton as the next President of the United States, and show the world we still believe in the promise of this great nation.

Thank you for this incredible journey. Let's keep it going. God bless the United States of America.

Dedication of the National Museum of African American History and Culture

NATIONAL MUSEUM OF AFRICAN AMERICAN
HISTORY AND CULTURE
WASHINGTON, D.C.
SATURDAY, SEPTEMBER 24, 2016

JAMES BALDWIN ONCE WROTE, "For while the tale of how we suffer, and how we are delighted, and how we may triumph is never new, it always must be heard." For while the tale of how we suffer, and how we are delighted, and how we may triumph is never new, it always must be heard.

Today, as so many generations have before, we gather on our National Mall to tell an essential part of our American story—one that has at times been overlooked—we come not just for today, but for all time.

President and Mrs. Bush; President Clinton; Vice President and Dr. Biden; Chief Justice Roberts; Secretary Skorton; Reverend Butts; distinguished guests: Thank you. Thank you for your leadership in making sure this tale is told. We're here in part because of you and because of all those Americans—the Civil War vets, the Civil Rights foot soldiers, the champions of this effort on Capitol Hill—who, for more than a century, kept the dream of this museum alive.

That includes our leaders in Congress—Paul Ryan and Nancy Pelosi. It includes one of my heroes, John Lewis, who, as he has so often, took the torch from those who came before him and brought us past the finish line. It includes the philanthropists and benefactors and advisory members who have so generously given not only their money but their time. It includes the Americans who offered up all the family keepsakes tucked away in Grandma's attic. And of course, it includes a man without whose vision and passion and persistence we would not be here today—Mr. Lonnie Bunch.

What we can see of this building—the towering glass, the artistry of the metalwork—is surely a sight to behold. But beyond the majesty of the building, what makes this occasion so special is the larger story it contains. Below us, this building reaches down seventy feet, its roots spreading far wider and deeper than any tree on this Mall. And on its lowest level, after you walk past remnants of a slave ship, after you reflect on the immortal declaration that "all men are created equal," you can see a block of stone. On top of this stone sits a historical marker, weathered by the ages. That marker reads: "General Andrew Jackson and Henry Clay spoke from this slave block…during the year 1830."

I want you to think about this. Consider what this artifact tells us about history, about how it's told, and about what can be cast aside. On a stone where day after day, for years, men and women were torn from their spouse or their child, shackled and bound, and bought and sold, and bid like cattle; on a stone worn down by the tragedy of over a thousand bare feet—for a long time, the only thing we considered important, the singular thing we once chose to commemorate as "history" with a plaque were the unmemorable speeches of two powerful men.

And that block I think explains why this museum is so necessary. Because that same object, reframed, put in context, tells us so much more. As Americans, we rightfully passed on the tales of the giants who built this country; who led armies into battle and waged seminal debates in the halls of Congress and the corridors of power. But too often, we ignored or forgot the stories of millions upon millions of others, who built this nation just as surely, whose humble eloquence, whose calloused hands, whose steady drive helped to create cities, erect industries, build the arsenals of democracy.

And so this national museum helps to tell a richer and fuller story of who we are. It helps us better understand the lives, yes, of the President, but also the slave; the industrialist, but also the porter; the keeper of the status quo, but also of the activist seeking to overthrow that status quo; the teacher or the cook, alongside the statesman. And by knowing this other story, we better understand ourselves and each other. It binds us together. It reaffirms that all of us are America—that African American history is not somehow separate from our larger American story, it's not the underside of the American story, it is central to the American story. That our glory derives not just from our most obvious triumphs, but how we've wrested triumph from tragedy, and how we've been able to remake ourselves, again and again and again, in accordance with our highest ideals.

I, too, am America.

The great historian John Hope Franklin, who helped to get this museum started, once said, "Good history is a good foundation for a better present and future." He understood the best history doesn't just sit behind a glass case; it helps us to understand what's outside the case. The best history helps us recognize the mistakes that we've made and the dark corners of the human spirit that we need to guard against. And, yes, a clear-eyed view of history can make us uncomfortable, and shake us out of familiar narratives. But it is precisely because of that discomfort that we learn and grow and harness our collective power to make this nation more perfect.

That's the American story that this museum tells— one of suffering and delight; one of fear but also of hope; of wandering in the wilderness and then seeing out on the horizon a glimmer of the Promised Land.

It is in this embrace of truth, as best as we can know it, in the celebration of the entire American experience, where real patriotism lies. As President Bush just said, a great nation doesn't shy from the truth. It strengthens us. It emboldens us. It should fortify us. It is an act of patriotism to understand where we've been. And this museum tells the story of so many patriots.

Yes, African Americans have felt the cold weight of shackles and the stinging lash of the field whip. But we've also dared to run north, and sing songs from Harriet Tubman's hymnal. We've buttoned up our Union Blues to join the fight for our freedom. We've railed against injustice for decade upon decade—a lifetime of struggle, and progress, and enlightenment that we see etched in Frederick Douglass's mighty, leonine gaze.

Yes, this museum tells a story of people who felt the indignity, the small and large humiliations of a "whites only" sign, or wept at the side of Emmett Till's coffin, or fell to their knees on shards of stained glass outside a church where four little girls died. But it also tells the story of the black youth and white youth sitting alongside each other, straight-backed, so full of dignity on those lunch counter stools; the story of a six-year-old Ruby Bridges, pigtails, fresh-pressed dress, walking that gauntlet to get to school; Tuskegee airmen soaring the skies not just to beat a dictator, but to reaffirm the promise of our democracy—but remind us that all of us are created equal.

This is the place to understand how protest and love of country don't merely coexist but inform each other; how men can proudly win the gold for their country but still insist on raising a black-gloved fist; how we can wear "I Can't Breathe" T-shirts and still grieve for fallen police officers. Here's the America where the razor-sharp uniform of the Chairman of the Joint Chiefs of Staff belongs alongside the cape of the Godfather of Soul. We have shown the world that we can float like butterflies and sting like bees; that we can rocket into space like Mae Jemison, steal home like Jackie, rock like Jimi, stir the pot like Richard Pryor; or we can be sick and tired of being sick and tired, like Fannie Lou Hamer, and still Rock Steady like Aretha Franklin.

We are large, Walt Whitman told us, containing multitudes. We are large, containing multitudes. Full of contradictions. That's America. That's what makes us grow. That's what makes us extraordinary. And as is true for America, so is true for the African American experience. We're not a burden on America, or a stain on America, or an object of pity or charity for America. We're America.

And that's what this museum explains—the fact that our stories have shaped every corner of our culture. The struggles for freedom that took place made our Constitution a real and living document, tested and shaped and deepened and made more profound its meaning for all people. The story told here doesn't just belong to black Americans; it belongs to all Americans—for the African American experience has been shaped just as much by Europeans and Asians and Native Americans and Latinos. We have informed each other. We are polyglot, a stew.

Scripture promised that if we lift up the oppressed, then our light will rise in the darkness, and our night will become like the noonday. And the story contained in this museum makes those words prophecy. And that's what this day is about. That's what this museum is about. I, too, am America. It is a glorious story, the one that's told here. It is complicated and it is messy and it is full of contradictions, as all great stories are, as Shakespeare is, as Scripture is. And it's a story that perhaps needs to be told now more than ever.

A museum alone will not alleviate poverty in every inner city or every rural hamlet. It won't eliminate gun violence from all our neighborhoods, or immediately ensure that justice is always colorblind. It won't wipe away every instance of discrimination in a job interview or a sentencing hearing or folks trying to rent an apartment. Those things are up to us, the decisions and choices we make. It requires speaking out, and organizing, and voting, until our values are fully reflected in our laws and our policies and our communities.

But what this museum does show us is that in even the face of oppression, even in the face of unimaginable difficulty, America has moved forward. And so this museum provides context for the debates of our times. It illuminates them and gives us some sense of how they evolved, and perhaps keeps them in proportion. Perhaps it can help a white visitor understand the pain and anger of demonstrators in places like Tulsa and Charlotte. But it can also help black visitors appreciate the fact that not only is this younger generation carrying on traditions of the past but, within the white communities across this nation we see the sincerity of law enforcement officers and officials who, in fits and starts, are struggling to understand, and are trying to do the right thing.

It reminds us that routine discrimination and Jim Crow aren't ancient history, it's just a blink in the eye of history. It was just yesterday. And so we should not be surprised that not all the healing is done. We shouldn't despair that it's not all solved. And knowing the larger story should instead remind us of just how remarkable the changes that have taken place truly are—just in my lifetime—and thereby inspire us to further progress.

And so hopefully this museum can help us talk to each other. And more importantly, listen to each other. And most importantly, see each other. Black and white and Latino and Native American and Asian American—see how our stories are bound together. And bound together with women in America, and workers in America, and entrepreneurs in America, and LGBT Americans. And for young people who didn't live through the struggles represented here, I hope you draw strength from the changes that have taken place. Come here and see the power of your own agency. See how young John Lewis was. These were children who transformed a nation in a blink of an eye. Young people, come here and see your ability to make your mark.

The very fact of this day does not prove that America is perfect, but it does validate the ideas of our founding, that this country born of change, this country born of revolution, this country of we, the people, this country can get better.

And that's why we celebrate, mindful that our work is not yet done; mindful that we are but on a waystation on this common journey towards freedom. And how glorious it is that we enshrine it here, on some of our nation's most hallowed ground—the same place where lives were once traded but also where hundreds of thousands of Americans, of all colors and creeds, once marched. How joyful it is that this story take its rightful place—alongside Jefferson who declared our independence, and Washington who made it real, and alongside Lincoln who saved our union, and the GIs who defended it; alongside a new monument to a King, gazing outward, summoning us toward that mountaintop. How righteous it is that we tell this story here.

For almost eight years, I have been blessed with the extraordinary honor of serving you in this office. Time and again, I've flown low over this Mall on Marine One, often with Michelle and our daughters. And President Clinton, President Bush, they'll tell you it is an incredible sight. We pass right across the Washington Monument—it feels like you can reach out and touch it. And at night, if you turn the other way, you don't just see the Lincoln Memorial, Old Abe is lit up and you can see him, his spirit glowing from that building. And we don't have many trips left. But over the years, I've always been comforted as I've watched this museum rise from this earth into this remarkable tribute. Because I know that years from now, like all of you, Michelle and I will be able to come here to this museum, and not just bring our kids but hopefully our grandkids. I imagine holding a little hand of somebody and tell[ing] them the stories that are enshrined here.

And in the years that follow, they'll be able to do the same. And then we'll go to the Lincoln Memorial and we'll take in the view atop the Washington Monument. And together, we'll learn about ourselves, as Americans—our sufferings, our delights, and our triumphs. And we'll walk away better for it, better because the better grasp of history. We'll walk away that much more in love with this country, the only place on Earth where this story could have unfolded.

It is a monument, no less than the others on this Mall, to the deep and abiding love for this country, and the ideals upon which it is founded. For we, too, are America.

So enough talk. President Bush is timing me. He had the over/under at twenty-five. Let us now open this museum to the world. Today, we have with us a family that reflects the arc of our progress: the Bonner family—four generations in all, starting with gorgeous seven-year-old Christine and going up to gorgeous ninety-nine-year-old Ruth.

Now, Ruth's father, Elijah Odom, was born into servitude in Mississippi. He was born a slave. As a young boy, he ran, though, to his freedom. He lived through Reconstruction and he lived through Jim Crow. But he went on to farm, and graduate from medical school, and gave life to the beautiful family that we see today—with a spirit reflected in beautiful Christine, free and equal in the laws of her country and in the eyes of God.

So in a brief moment, their family will join us in ringing a bell from the First Baptist Church in Virginia—one of the oldest black churches in America, founded under a grove of trees in 1776. And the sound of this bell will be echoed by others in houses of worship and town squares all across this country—an echo of the ringing bells that signaled Emancipation more than a century and a half ago; the sound, and the anthem, of American freedom.

God bless you all. God bless the United States of America.

Farewell Address

McCORMICK PLACE
CHICAGO, ILLINOIS
TUESDAY, JANUARY 10, 2017

IT'S GOOD TO BE HOME. My fellow Americans, Michelle and I have been so touched by all the well-wishes we've received over the past few weeks. But tonight it's my turn to say thanks. Whether we've seen eye-to-eye or rarely agreed at all, my conversations with you, the American people—in living rooms and schools; at farms and on factory floors; at diners and on distant outposts—are what have kept me honest, kept me inspired, and kept me going. Every day, I learned from you. You made me a better President, and you made me a better man.

I first came to Chicago when I was in my early twenties, still trying to figure out who I was; still searching for a purpose to my life. It was in neighborhoods not far from here where I began working with church groups in the shadows of closed steel mills. It was on these streets where I witnessed the power of faith, and the quiet dignity of working people in the face of struggle and loss. This is where I learned that change only happens when ordinary people get involved, get engaged, and come together to demand it.

After eight years as your President, I still believe that. And it's not just my belief. It's the beating heart of our American idea—our bold experiment in self-government.

It's the conviction that we are all created equal, endowed by our Creator with certain unalienable rights, among them life, liberty, and the pursuit of happiness.

It's the insistence that these rights, while self-evident, have never been self-executing; that We, the People, through the instrument of our democracy, can form a more perfect union.

This is the great gift our Founders gave us. The freedom to chase our individual dreams through our sweat, toil, and imagination—and the imperative to strive together as well, to achieve a greater good.

For 240 years, our nation's call to citizenship has given work and purpose to each new generation. It's what led patriots to choose republic over tyranny, pioneers to trek west, slaves to brave that makeshift railroad to freedom. It's what pulled immigrants and refugees across oceans and the Rio Grande, pushed women to reach for the ballot, powered workers to organize. It's why GIs gave their lives at Omaha Beach and Iwo Jima; Iraq and Afghanistan—and why men and women from Selma to Stonewall were prepared to give theirs as well.

So that's what we mean when we say America is exceptional. Not that our nation has been flawless from the start, but that we have shown the capacity to change, and make life better for those who follow.

Yes, our progress has been uneven. The work of democracy has always been hard, contentious and sometimes bloody. For every two steps forward, it often feels we take one step back. But the long sweep of America has been defined by forward motion, a constant widening of our founding creed to embrace all, and not just some.

If I had told you eight years ago that America would reverse a great recession, reboot our auto industry, and unleash the longest stretch of job creation in our history...if I had told you that we would open up a new chapter with the Cuban people, shut down Iran's nuclear weapons program without firing a shot, and take out the mastermind of 9/11...if I had told you that we would win marriage equality, and secure the right to health insurance for another 20 million of our fellow citizens—you might have said our sights were set a little too high.

But that's what we did. That's what you did. You were the change. You answered people's hopes, and because of you, by almost every measure, America is a better, stronger place than it was when we started.

In ten days, the world will witness a hallmark of our democracy: the peaceful transfer of power from one freely elected president to the next. I committed to President-Elect Trump that my administration would ensure the smoothest possible transition, just as President Bush did for me. Because it's up to all of us to make sure our government can help us meet the many challenges we still face.

We have what we need to do so. After all, we remain the wealthiest, most powerful, and most respected nation on Earth. Our youth and drive, our diversity and openness, our boundless capacity for risk and reinvention mean that the future should be ours.

But that potential will be realized only if our democracy works. Only if our politics reflects the decency of our people. Only if all of us, regardless of our party affiliation or particular interest, help restore the sense of common purpose that we so badly need right now.

That's what I want to focus on tonight—the state of our democracy.

Understand, democracy does not require uniformity. Our founders quarreled and compromised, and expected us to do the same. But they knew that democracy does require a basic sense of solidarity—the idea that for all our outward differences, we are all in this together; that we rise or fall as one.

There have been moments throughout our history that threatened to rupture that solidarity. The beginning of this century has been one of those times. A shrinking world, growing inequality; demographic change and the specter of terrorism—these forces haven't just tested our security and prosperity, but our democracy as well. And how we meet these challenges to our democracy will determine our ability to educate our kids, and create good jobs, and protect our homeland.

In other words, it will determine our future.

Our democracy won't work without a sense that everyone has economic opportunity. Today, the economy is growing again; wages, incomes, home values, and retirement accounts are rising again; poverty is falling again. The wealthy are paying a fairer share of taxes even as the stock market shatters records. The unemployment rate is near a ten-year low. The uninsured rate has never, ever been lower. Health care costs are rising at the slowest rate in fifty years. And if anyone can put together a plan that is demonstrably better than the improvements we've made to our health care system—that covers as many people at less cost—I will publicly support it.

That, after all, is why we serve—to make people's lives better, not worse.

But for all the real progress we've made, we know it's not enough. Our economy doesn't work as well or grow as fast when a few prosper at the expense of a growing middle class. But stark inequality is also corrosive to our democratic principles. While the top 1 percent has amassed a bigger share of wealth and income, too many families, in inner cities and rural counties, have been left behind—the laid-off factory worker; the waitress and health care worker who struggle to pay the bills—convinced that the game is fixed against them, that their government only serves the interests of the powerful—a recipe for more cynicism and polarization in our politics.

There are no quick fixes to this long-term trend. I agree that our trade should be fair and not just free. But the next wave of economic dislocation won't come from overseas. It will come from the relentless pace of automation that makes many good, middle-class jobs obsolete.

And so we must forge a new social compact—to guarantee all our kids the education they need; to give workers the power to unionize for better wages; to update the social safety net to reflect the way we live now and make more reforms to the tax code so corporations and individuals who reap the most from the new economy don't avoid their obligations to the country that's made their success possible. We can argue about how to best achieve these goals. But we can't be complacent about the goals themselves. For if we don't create opportunity for all people, the disaffection and division that has stalled our progress will only sharpen in years to come.

There's a second threat to our democracy—one as old as our nation itself. After my election, there was talk of a post-racial America. Such a vision, however well-intended, was never realistic. For race remains a potent and often divisive force in our society. I've lived long enough to know that race relations are better than they were ten, or twenty, or thirty years ago—you can see it not just in statistics, but in the attitudes of young Americans across the political spectrum.

But we're not where we need to be. All of us have more work to do. After all, if every economic issue is framed as a struggle between a hardworking white middle class and undeserving minorities, then workers of all shades will be left fighting for scraps while the wealthy withdraw further into their private enclaves. If we decline to invest in the children of immigrants, just because they don't look like us, we diminish the prospects of our own children—because those brown kids will represent a larger share of America's workforce. And our economy doesn't have to be a zero-sum game. Last year, incomes rose for all races, all age groups, for men and for women.

Going forward, we must uphold laws against discrimination—in hiring, in housing, in education and the criminal justice system. That's what our Constitution and highest ideals require. But laws alone won't be enough. Hearts must change. If our democracy is to work in this increasingly diverse nation, each one of us must try to heed the advice of one of the great characters in American fiction, Atticus Finch, who said, "You never really understand a person until you consider things from his point of view…until you climb into his skin and walk around in it."

For blacks and other minorities, it means tying our own struggles for justice to the challenges that a lot of people in this country face—the refugee, the immigrant, the rural poor, the transgender American, and also the middle-aged white man who from the outside may seem like he's got all the advantages, but who's seen his world upended by economic, cultural, and technological change.

For white Americans, it means acknowledging that the effects of slavery and Jim Crow didn't suddenly vanish in the '60s; that when minority groups voice discontent, they're not just engaging in reverse racism or practicing political correctness; that when they wage peaceful protest, they're not demanding special treatment, but the equal treatment our Founders promised.

For native-born Americans, it means reminding ourselves that the stereotypes about immigrants today were said, almost word for word, about the Irish, Italians, and Poles. America wasn't weakened by the presence of these newcomers; they embraced this nation's creed, and it was strengthened.

So regardless of the station we occupy, we have to try harder; to start with the premise that each of our fellow citizens loves this country just as much as we do; that they value hard work and family like we do; that their children are just as curious and hopeful and worthy of love as our own.

None of this is easy. For too many of us, it's become safer to retreat into our own bubbles, whether in our neighborhoods or college campuses or places of worship or our social media feeds, surrounded by people who look like us and share the same political outlook and never challenge our assumptions. The rise of naked partisanship, increasing economic and regional stratification, the splintering of our media into a channel for every taste—all this makes this great sorting seem natural, even inevitable. And increasingly, we become so secure in our bubbles that we accept only information, whether true or not, that fits our opinions, instead of basing our opinions on the evidence that's out there.

This trend represents a third threat to our democracy. Politics is a battle of ideas; in the course of a healthy debate, we'll prioritize different goals, and the different means of reaching them. But without some common baseline of facts; without a willingness to admit new information, and concede that your opponent is making a fair point, and that science and reason matter, we'll keep talking past each other, making common ground and compromise impossible.

Isn't that part of what makes politics so dispiriting? How can elected officials rage about deficits when we propose to spend money on preschool for kids, but not when we're cutting taxes for corporations? How do we excuse ethical lapses in our own party, but pounce when the other party does the same thing? It's not just dishonest, this selective sorting of the facts; it's self-defeating. Because as my mother used to tell me, reality has a way of catching up with you.

Take the challenge of climate change. In just eight years, we've halved our dependence on foreign oil, doubled our renewable energy, and led the world to an agreement that has the promise to save this planet. But without bolder action, our children won't have time to debate the existence of climate change; they'll be busy dealing with its effects: environmental disasters, economic disruptions, and waves of climate refugees seeking sanctuary.

Now, we can and should argue about the best approach to the problem. But to simply deny the problem not only betrays future generations; it betrays the essential spirit of innovation and practical problem-solving that guided our Founders.

It's that spirit, born of the Enlightenment, that made us an economic powerhouse—the spirit that took flight at Kitty Hawk and Cape Canaveral; the spirit that cures disease and put a computer in every pocket.

It's that spirit—a faith in reason, and enterprise, and the primacy of right over might, that allowed us to resist the lure of fascism and tyranny during the Great Depression, and build a post–World War II order with other democracies, an order based not just on military power or national affiliations but on principles—the rule of law, human rights, freedoms of religion, speech, assembly, and an independent press.

That order is now being challenged—first by violent fanatics who claim to speak for Islam; more recently by autocrats in foreign capitals who see free markets, open democracies, and civil society itself as a threat to their power. The peril each poses to our democracy is more far-reaching than a car bomb or a missile. It represents the fear of change; the fear of people who look or speak or pray differently; a contempt for the rule of law that holds leaders accountable; an intolerance of dissent and free thought; a belief that the sword or the gun or the bomb or propaganda machine is the ultimate arbiter of what's true and what's right.

Because of the extraordinary courage of our men and women in uniform, and the intelligence officers, law enforcement, and diplomats who support them, no foreign terrorist organization has successfully planned and executed an attack on our homeland these past eight years; and although Boston and Orlando remind us of how dangerous radicalization can be, our law enforcement agencies are more effective and vigilant than ever. We've taken out tens of thousands of terrorists—including Osama bin Laden. The global coalition we're leading against ISIL has taken out their leaders, and taken away about half their territory. ISIL will be destroyed, and no one who threatens America will ever be safe. To all who serve, it has been the honor of my lifetime to be your Commander-in-Chief.

But protecting our way of life requires more than our military. Democracy can buckle when we give in to fear. So just as we, as citizens, must remain vigilant against external aggression, we must guard against a weakening of the values that make us who we are. That's why, for the past eight years, I've worked to put the fight against terrorism on a firm legal footing. That's why we've ended torture, worked to close Gitmo, and reform our laws governing surveillance to protect privacy and civil liberties. That's why I reject discrimination against Muslim Americans. That's why we cannot withdraw from global fights—to expand democracy, and human rights, women's rights, and LGBT rights—no matter how imperfect our efforts, no matter how expedient ignoring such values may seem. For the fight against extremism and intolerance and sectarianism are of a piece with the fight against authoritarianism and nationalist aggression. If the scope of freedom and respect for the rule of law shrinks around the world, the likelihood of war within and between nations increases, and our own freedoms will eventually be threatened.

So let's be vigilant, but not afraid. ISIL will try to kill innocent people. But they cannot defeat America unless we betray our Constitution and our principles in the fight. Rivals like Russia or China cannot match our influence around the world—unless we give up what we stand for, and turn ourselves into just another big country that bullies smaller neighbors.

Which brings me to my final point—our democracy is threatened whenever we take it for granted. All of us, regardless of party, should throw ourselves into the task of rebuilding our democratic institutions. When voting rates are some of the lowest among advanced democracies, we should make it easier, not harder, to vote. When trust in our institutions is low, we should reduce the corrosive influence of money in our politics, and insist on the principles of transparency and ethics in public service. When Congress is dysfunctional, we should draw our districts to encourage politicians to cater to common sense and not rigid extremes.

And all of this depends on our participation; on each of us accepting the responsibility of citizenship, regardless of which way the pendulum of power swings.

Our Constitution is a remarkable, beautiful gift. But it's really just a piece of parchment. It has no power on its own. We, the people, give it power—with our participation, and the choices we make. Whether or not we stand up for our freedoms. Whether or not we respect and enforce the rule of law. America is no fragile thing. But the gains of our long journey to freedom are not assured.

In his own farewell address, George Washington wrote that self-government is the underpinning of our safety, prosperity, and liberty, but "from different causes and from different quarters much pains will be taken…to weaken in your minds the conviction of this truth;" that we should preserve it with "jealous anxiety;" that we should reject "the first dawning of every attempt to alienate any portion of our country from the rest or to enfeeble the sacred ties" that make us one.

We weaken those ties when we allow our political dialogue to become so corrosive that people of good character are turned off from public service; so coarse with rancor that Americans with whom we disagree are not just misguided, but somehow malevolent. We weaken those ties when we define some of us as more American than others; when we write off the whole system as inevitably corrupt, and blame the leaders we elect without examining our own role in electing them.

It falls to each of us to be those anxious, jealous guardians of our democracy; to embrace the joyous task we've been given to continually try to improve this great nation of ours. Because for all our outward differences, we all share the same proud title: Citizen.

Ultimately, that's what our democracy demands. It needs you. Not just when there's an election, not just when your own narrow interest is at stake, but over the full span of a lifetime. If you're tired of arguing with strangers on the Internet, try to talk with one in real life. If something needs fixing, lace up your shoes and do some organizing. If you're disappointed by your elected officials, grab a clipboard, get some signatures, and run for office yourself. Show up. Dive in. Persevere. Sometimes you'll win. Sometimes you'll lose. Presuming a reservoir of goodness in others can be a risk, and there will be times when the process disappoints you. But for those of us fortunate enough to have been a part of this work, to see it up close, let me tell you, it can energize and inspire. And more often than not, your faith in America—and in Americans—will be confirmed.

Mine sure has been. Over the course of these eight years, I've seen the hopeful faces of young graduates and our newest military officers. I've mourned with grieving families searching for answers, and found grace in a Charleston church. I've seen our scientists help a paralyzed man regain his sense of touch, and our wounded warriors walk again. I've seen our doctors and volunteers rebuild after earthquakes and stop pandemics in their tracks. I've seen the youngest of children remind us of our obligations to care for refugees, to work in peace, and above all to look out for each other.

That faith I placed all those years ago, not far from here, in the power of ordinary Americans to bring about change—that faith has been rewarded in ways I couldn't possibly have imagined. I hope yours has, too. Some of you here tonight or watching at home were there with us in 2004, in 2008, in 2012—and maybe you still can't believe we pulled this whole thing off.

You're not the only ones. Michelle—for the past twenty-five years, you've been not only my wife and mother of my children, but my best friend. You took on a role you didn't ask for and made it your own with grace and grit and style and good humor. You made the White House a place that belongs to everybody. And a new generation sets its sights higher because it has you as a role model. You've made me proud. You've made the country proud.

Malia and Sasha, under the strangest of circumstances, you have become two amazing young women, smart and beautiful, but more importantly, kind and thoughtful and full of passion. You wore the burden of years in the spotlight so easily. Of all that I've done in my life, I'm most proud to be your dad. To Joe Biden, the scrappy kid from Scranton who became Delaware's favorite son: you were the first choice I made as a nominee, and the best. Not just because you have been a great Vice President, but because in the bargain, I gained a brother. We love you and Jill like family, and your friendship has been one of the great joys of our life.

To my remarkable staff: For eight years—and for some of you, a whole lot more—I've drawn from your energy, and tried to reflect back what you displayed every day: heart, and character, and idealism. I've watched you grow up, get married, have kids, and start incredible new journeys of your own. Even when times got tough and frustrating, you never let Washington get the better of you. The only thing that makes me prouder than all the good we've done is the thought of all the remarkable things you'll achieve from here.

And to all of you out there—every organizer who moved to an unfamiliar town and kind family who welcomed them in, every volunteer who knocked on doors, every young person who cast a ballot for the first time, every American who lived and breathed the hard work of change—you are the best supporters and organizers anyone could hope for, and I will forever be grateful. Because yes, you changed the world.

That's why I leave this stage tonight even more optimistic about this country than I was when we started. Because I know our work has not only helped so many Americans; it has inspired so many Americans—especially so many young people out there—to believe you can make a difference; to hitch your wagon to something bigger than yourselves. This generation coming up—unselfish, altruistic, creative, patriotic—I've seen you in every corner of the country. You believe in a fair, just, inclusive America; you know that constant change has been America's hallmark, something not to fear but to embrace, and you are willing to carry this hard work of democracy forward. You'll soon outnumber any of us, and I believe as a result that the future is in good hands.

My fellow Americans, it has been the honor of my life to serve you. I won't stop; in fact, I will be right there with you, as a citizen, for all my days that remain. For now, whether you're young or young at heart, I do have one final ask of you as your President—the same thing I asked when you took a chance on me eight years ago.

I am asking you to believe. Not in my ability to bring about change—but in yours.

I am asking you to hold fast to that faith written into our founding documents; that idea whispered by slaves and abolitionists; that spirit sung by immigrants and homesteaders and those who marched for justice; that creed reaffirmed by those who planted flags from foreign battlefields to the surface of the moon; a creed at the core of every American whose story is not yet written:

Yes We Can.

Yes We Did.

Yes We Can.

Thank you. God bless you. And may God continue to bless the United States of America.

CPSIA information can be obtained
at www.ICGtesting.com
Printed in the USA
BVHW03s1913220618
519801BV00001B/17/P